T0279317

TEXAS
BLUEGRASS
LEGACIES

TEXAS
BLUEGRASS
LEGACIES

FAMILIES AND MENTORS
THROUGH THE GENERATIONS

Jeff Campbell and Braeden Paul

Foreword by Alan Munde

THE
History
PRESS

Published by The History Press
Charleston, SC
www.historypress.com

First published 2023

Manufactured in the United States

ISBN 9781467153676

Library of Congress Control Number: 2023932156

Notice: The information in this book is true and complete to the best of our knowledge. It is offered without guarantee on the part of the authors or The History Press. The authors and The History Press disclaim all liability in connection with the use of this book.

CONTENTS

Foreword, by Alan Munde   9
Preface, by Jeff Campbell   13
Acknowledgements   15
Introduction, by Braeden Paul   17

Riley Gilbreath   21

PART I. FAMILIES
Banjo Ben and the Purple Hulls   29
The Cooke Brothers   39
Born in Texas   43
Jesse Brock (C.W. Brock Family)   47
The Davis Brothers (Greg and Brad)   51
Chuck Lee: Santa Makes Banjos   55
The Pyeatt Family   57
The Steel Drivin' Fiddler   60
The Vestal Brothers (Scott and Curtis)   65
The Whites   69

PART II. MENTORS
A Dawg and a Herd of Longhorns   77
Camp Bluegrass at South Plains College   87
High Plains Jamboree   94

CONTENTS

From Grapeland to Austin: An Interview with Andi Jo Huff   98
The Lone Star Guitar Prodigy   104
Pickin' on the Square   107
Jade Throneberry's Full Plate   111
Play It Forward   116

Notes   119
About the Authors   127

Play It Forward

This book is dedicated to the loving memory of Professor Rod Moag. His research on bluegrass music in Texas as well as his assistance on our first book, Texas Bluegrass History, *will forever be appreciated by us.*

—*Braeden Paul and Jeff Campbell*

FOREWORD

Thank you, Texas.

I was born in Norman, Oklahoma. I became interested in music in my very early teens and began to learn to play the guitar first and then the banjo from players and teachers in the Norman and Oklahoma City area. It was during my freshman and sophomore years in college at the University of Oklahoma that I met and played with musicians from different parts of the country. Very prominent among them was the world-class fiddler Byron Berline. Raised on a farm in Oklahoma near Caldwell, Kansas, Byron was two years ahead of me in school and, at the time I met him, had already won the National Fiddle Championship at the Weiser, Idaho contest; recorded with the Dillards; and appeared, along with his father, Lou Berline, at the prestigious Newport Folk Festival, where he met and played with Bill Monroe. He later went on to work and record with Monroe.

Byron was one of my most exciting and most immediate conduits to the outside world of bluegrass music. Through his accomplishments and connections, I became aware of many bluegrass musicians, bands, songs, styles and ways of relating to the music that, had I been left to my own devices, would have taken me several years, if ever, to discover.

Among his many connections in the seemingly underground world of bluegrass music was that to the Texas bluegrass pickers. Among them were mandolin player and singer Mitchell Land and the superb banjo player Eddie Shelton. There were others, but those two were the important ones for me.

Alan Munde (*pointing*) with Byron Berline, Roger Bush and Roland White in Dripping Springs, Texas, October 11, 2016. *Photo courtesy of Rick Gardner.*

When I was growing up in Oklahoma, Texas was the looming giant to the south. Our house was near the University of Oklahoma and, in turn, the football stadium. The number-one opponent and feared and hated football rival was the University of Texas. It seemed not only my focus but that of the whole state was south toward Texas. Oklahoma shared borders with other states, but there was only one Red River.

Eddie Shelton was born in Tennessee but was raised in the Dallas, Texas area. He worked for the National Cash Register Company and had been assigned to the Oklahoma City office. Byron, still a student at OU, met him and began playing with Eddie as part of the band on the Bill Snow and Sonny Woodring country music TV show on an Oklahoma City station. I would watch and listen to them every Saturday afternoon, mostly Eddie, and try to pick up on the fine art of bluegrass and banjo picking. I didn't have a car but talked a friend into driving to Oklahoma City to hear the group at the Oklahoma State Fair. Byron later introduced me to Eddie. Eddie took me under his wing, as he did many others over his lifetime, and helped me become a much better player than I would have been without his help.

After meeting Eddie and also Mitchell Land, I would travel by bus down to the Dallas area for a weekend away from school to play music with Mitchell and others in his music circle. Later, when Eddie moved back to the Dallas area, I would continue to bus myself down to pick music and continue to pick Eddie's brain. Those days were some of the very best in my life. I learned a whole bunch about bluegrass and bluegrass banjo in particular.

During my musical career, Texas was always there. The very first person I met when I moved to Nashville to work for Jimmy Martin was Houstonian and banjo player Tony Ullrich, who put me up for several days. We kept in touch after he moved back to Houston. The group I performed and recorded with for many years, California-based Country Gazette, played many, many dates in the Lone Star State. As bandmates left, we recruited several very wonderful players from Texas: Joe Carr, Mike Anderson, Dave Ferguson, Bill Honker, Glenn Mitchell, Phill Elliott, Elliott Rogers and others. We leaned on our Texas bluegrass friendships for places to stay. Doc Hamilton, a skillful and knowledgeable player of all the bluegrass instruments, offered us many a fine time. Rick Gardner, a banjo-playing photographer of high reputation and skill, took several of our promotional photos, along with those of many other national traveling acts. Dennis McDaniel, everyone's bluegrass buddy, was a source of sparkling good times of music making. They were many Texans who helped our way along the trail.

During later times and after my band years, I taught for twenty years at one of the very first colleges to offer studies in bluegrass music, South Plains College, Levelland, Texas. After leaving there, I lived twenty years in the Wimberley, Texas area and bathed in the music of the many talented bluegrass artists in the Austin and San Antonio area. Texas has been very kind to me and to many other bluegrass musicians, as *Texas Bluegrass Legacies: Families and Mentors through the Generations* so amply illustrates. Again, thank you, Texas.

Alan Munde

PREFACE

"As long as I can remember I've wanted to make a record with my dad.
He's the one who taught me how to play."
—Billy Strings[1]

As a guitarist, Billy Strings is a generational talent, but even extremely gifted musicians need mentorship and guidance to get started. For Billy, it was his father, Terry Barber, who taught him to play guitar. In November 2022, Billy released the album *Me / and / Dad*, a collaboration and tribute to the man who got him started.

Jeff Campbell with Dallas music historian Roy Wood. "Uncle" Roy has given away dozens of musical instruments to aspiring musicians. The consummate example of "play it forward." *Photo courtesy of the Kanikapila Island Strummers.*

That's really what this book is about: families and mentors, as they relate to the Texas bluegrass scene. It could easily be another state or another subject. There could be books like this one on Oregon fishermen, Massachusetts artists or Colorado cowboys and cowgirls.[2] Because most all of us have found success due to our families or mentors.

As I get older, I think of my family and my mentors and what they have taught me. Some of them have passed on, and the best thing I can do is pass on the things they have taught me. Because without them, I probably would not be writing these words right now.

Jeff Campbell

ACKNOWLEDGEMENTS

Braeden Paul Would Like to Thank

My father, Robby Paul, and grandfather Bobby Paul for introducing me to this big part of my life called bluegrass music.

My mother, Michelle Hammock, for constantly seeing my potential and making sure others saw it as well.

David, Diana, Zack, Adam, Lindsay, Jared and all of my family for their love and support.

John Lawless and Terry Herd of *Bluegrass Today* for giving me a chance to exercise my writing muscle on a weekly basis.

The Southwest Bluegrass Club for their tireless promotion of bluegrass music and their support of my endeavors.

All of the individuals who gave their time and resources for the book.

Jeff Campbell for being a great collaborator and guiding me through the book writing process.

Jeff Campbell Would Like to Thank

My wife for her love, encouragement and support.

Alan Tompkins and the Bluegrass Heritage Foundation for treating us like family.

Alan Munde for being an encouraging mentor and writing the foreword for this book.

The Central Texas Bluegrass Association for its enthusiastic support.

Rick Gardner and Liz Patton for their wonderful photos.

All of the talented musicians who gave their time to be interviewed for this book.

My coauthor, Braeden Paul, for agreeing to take on the challenge of writing a book, one more time!

INTRODUCTION

When Jeff Campbell and I began making plans to write a follow-up to *Texas Bluegrass History: High Lonesome on the High Plains*, we decided that this next book needed to focus on a singular aspect of the bluegrass genre. When thinking about what to delve into, I couldn't help but reflect on my own background. Although I was born in Baton Rouge, Louisiana, I've spent the majority of my existence in the state of Texas.

For as long as I can remember, bluegrass music has always been part of my life. Some of my earliest memories involve hearing my father, Robby Paul, play his banjo around our home. There was also his collection of live VHS tapes with artists like Earl Scruggs, J.D. Crowe and Del McCoury that I watched on a regular basis. Of course there were also recordings he and I listened to frequently such as *At the Old Schoolhouse* by the Johnson Mountain Boys and the Rounder Records compilation *Blue Ribbon Bluegrass*.

After I learned to play mandolin at age fifteen, he and I would play music with each other on a regular basis, eventually performing and recording as part of several groups in the Dallas area. Several of our former band mates also guided me on my journey such as Jim Rozell, who gave an inexperienced seventeen-year-old his first opportunity to perform in front of an audience as part of Blackland Grass. Buzz Busby of Blue Valley Bluegrass not only taught me about presentation and showmanship, but he also helped me acquire my first professional-grade mandolin. Richard Suddreth, Joe Morrow, Pamela Dahl and Philip Ferguson were others who helped me further my abilities as a performing musician.

Top: Blue Valley Bluegrass circa 2014. *Standing*: Joe Morrow and Buzz Busby; *seated*: Braeden Paul, Robby Paul and Pamela Dahl. *Photo courtesy of Dotty Busby.*

Bottom: Braeden Paul and his father, Robby, performing together at the Jim Paul Miller Memorial Bluegrass Show in Garland, Texas. Their musical duo is known as the Flathead Fords. *Photo courtesy of Joshua Adkisson.*

Another early influence was my grandpa on my dad's side of the family, Bobby Paul. Like my dad had done for me, my grandpa (or Pawpaw as the grandkids refer to him) had introduced him to this music when he was growing up in Alexandria, Louisiana. In recent conversations with my father, he remembers hearing Pawpaw play banjo, fiddle and occasionally guitar around the house. As he still does even today, my grandpa had a vast collection of records. This is where my dad was introduced to pioneering artists such as Bill Monroe, Flatt and Scruggs and the Stanley Brothers, among others. I would eventually hear some of these recordings myself.

Pawpaw had a direct hand in two of the most pivotal moments in my life. One was when he introduced me to the music of Doyle Lawson, one of my greatest inspirations as a mandolinist. The other was when he handed me a copy of the Bill Monroe biography, *Can't You Hear Me Callin'*, by Richard D. Smith. Although I've always had a love for the genre, that book ignited within me a passion to explore the history of bluegrass music. I wanted to learn as much as I could about the people who played it, sang it and, at times, traveled difficult roads to share it with others. It's a quest I'm still on today.

My story is not terribly uncommon compared to others within the bluegrass community. There's actually quite a few parallels within the stories of myself, my father and my grandfather. Although bluegrass itself hadn't fully come into existence in his early years, Pawpaw was introduced to old-time string band music by his father, Robert "Bokey" Paul. Containing similar elements to bluegrass music, old-time is considered a precursor to the genre. It's what my great-grandfather specialized in when he played fiddle on radio stations around Louisiana as a young man. Just as Pawpaw had been for me, Bokey was also an early influence on my father's musical journey. Dad has often spoken of him and his grandpa sitting around playing tunes together on fiddle and banjo such as "Ragtime Annie," "Bully of the Town" and "Leather Britches," among others.

My story, as well as the others you'll read in this book, illustrates how a traditionally oriented genre such as bluegrass has continually thrived. Whether it was a family member or a neighboring elder, these folks willingly introduced this music to future generations, ensuring that it would always be cherished and enjoyed. Jeff and I both feel it's important to tip our hats not only to talented Texas bluegrass musicians but also to those who led them to their respective paths.

Braeden Paul

RILEY GILBREATH

W e begin this book with an artist whose story embodies both family ties to music and the influence of several mentors.

On June 25, 2022, in Wylie, Texas, a youthful banjoist named Riley Gilbreath and his band Lone Star Blue took the stage at the Bluegrass on Ballard festival to present their driving brand of bluegrass to the festival's patrons. The event hosted by the Bluegrass Heritage Foundation played a vital role in Gilbreath's musical journey going back to the very beginning.

Riley Gilbreath was born on April 12, 2004, and has spent all of his life in the town of Crowley, a suburb of Fort Worth, Texas. His parents also grew up in the state, but his mother, Jana, was born in Oklahoma. Her family, the VanBebers, would eventually relocate to Texas.

Although Riley himself didn't become interested in music until he was twelve years old, his family had a pretty good bit of musical history themselves. Jana and her family performed as a gospel group known as the Singing Vans (short for the family name, VanBeber). Their repertoire was primarily centered on traditional hymns, and they would often have a piano player for accompaniment. Interestingly enough, two of Riley's great-grandfathers on his mom's side of the family, Elmer Leonard and Jim Land, played banjo, a fact that he wasn't aware of until he started playing the instrument. His great-grandmother Gladys Land also played guitar and sang.

Riley's great-grandfather on his dad's side of the family Ralph Aiello was a West Virginia coal miner who played guitar and sang on radio stations around the area. He would eventually make his way to Texas due to his diagnosis with coal workers' pneumoconiosis (most commonly known as black lung). Eventually, Riley would inherit his family's musical interests.

Riley's musical journey began in 2016 after hearing a recording that featured a banjo: "I think it might've been Joey + Rory. There might've been a record or a song that had a banjo or something that I heard."[3]

Soon after that, the young boy showed interest in learning how to play the five-string instrument. His father, Danny, got in touch with the Bluegrass Heritage Foundation, which provided Riley with a loaner banjo through their Play It Forward program to get him started.

The Play It Forward program also helped Gilbreath come into contact with Jim Penson, a luthier and bluegrass instrument instructor in Arlington, Texas. Penson recalls this stage of Riley's musical journey: "At first, he was this shy kid who would barely talk. With new young students, I never know who is going to 'catch fire' or not. With Riley, it happened one day when he walked in and he could play 'Cripple Creek' successfully. I could see the lightbulb go off over his head."[4]

As Riley progressed on the banjo, his interest in bluegrass music got deeper and deeper. According to Penson, "His dad, Danny, would tell me that Riley had gone to sleep with the banjo around his neck."[5]

His parents were very supportive of their young son's newfound love of bluegrass music, taking him to jams and festivals on just about every weekend. As Riley remembers, "He [Jim] told me to go out and play with people 'cause that's how you get better. There was the first Saturday jam out at Pearl, Texas, at the old schoolhouse, so we started going to that. On the second Saturday we'd go to the Lillian Baptist Church, they had a jam out there. Then there was the third Saturday jam in Oakdale Park. That's where I really got my roots of pickin' with those kind of people and learning those songs."[6]

His formal lessons with Jim Penson and all the many jams Riley took part in caused his banjo playing to advance very rapidly. This would catch the attention of noted banjo builder Steve Huber, who would become aware of Riley's prowess at the 2017 Bloomin' Bluegrass Festival in Farmers Branch, Texas. It was then that Steve along with Alan Tompkins, the founder of the Bluegrass Heritage Foundation, decided that Gilbreath needed to have a Huber Workhorse banjo. The instrument was a professional-grade model that at the time sold for more than $3,000. In an act of generosity, Huber agreed to sell it for a price that the Play It Forward program and Riley's parents could both afford.[7] The banjo was presented to Riley on stage later that evening.

Left: Riley Gilbreath with his banjo teacher Jim Penson at Oakdale Park in Glen Rose, Texas. *Photo courtesy of Riley Gilbreath.*

Right: Riley Gilbreath with Steve Huber. Huber built the banjo that Gilbreath primarily uses on stage. *Photo courtesy of Riley Gilbreath.*

In 2018 at the age of fourteen, Riley would begin the performance side of his career as the banjoist for Dale Brawner's band Cedar Junction. Brawner was responsible for the monthly bluegrass jam and show that Riley had attended at the Lillian Baptist Church, located in a small unincorporated community in Johnston County. Dale was a known presence at bluegrass events in Texas and was particularly encouraging toward younger students of the music. "He made a big impact on my life definitely. I will say he was a great bandleader. Even leading my own band, I think back to some of the ways that he would lead the band to help myself out. He was a great influence on me," Riley recalled.[8] That same year Gilbreath was named the Oklahoma state banjo champion.

Also during that same time frame, Riley would begin learning the bluegrass style of guitar. He was largely influenced by the music of two brothers who hailed from Dickenson County, Virginia, Ralph and Carter Stanley: "I picked up guitar and I started listening to the Stanley Brothers a lot, and I would learn little simple guitar breaks in the songs and the intros. That's where my guitar roots are."[9]

Cedar Junction. *From left to right*: Riley Gilbreath, Joy Brawner, Jim Chapman, Dale Brawner, Caren Chapman and Darrell Lambert. *Photo courtesy of Riley Gilbreath.*

This skill would ultimately come in handy for Gilbreath as he would soon become the lead guitarist for the band Pocket Change. A couple of months prior to Riley joining them, his father, Danny, had become a member of the group as a rhythm guitarist and vocalist. Both Gilbreaths would perform with the group for the next two years.

The year 2019 was monumental for Riley. On top of performing regularly with Pocket Change, he won that year's Texas State Banjo Championship and also earned the title of Oklahoma state banjo champion for the second year.

In 2021 Riley would receive a call from bassist Anji Pearl that would usher in the next chapter of his music career: "She was throwing a festival at Oakdale Park and she had asked me to throw a band together to go play there, so I asked a couple of guys. At the time it was Alan Tompkins on bass and then Cole Gore and Sam Smith, who are still in the band now, they played guitar and mandolin, and Bryan Hollifield, he played banjo. I played guitar at the first two shows, and Ramey Moore was on fiddle."[10]

Shortly after the new band made their debut at the Pearl of a Jam Festival in Glen Rose, Texas, Riley Gilbreath also made an inaugural appearance at

Riley Gilbreath and Lone Star Blue. *From left to right*: Sam Smith, Leah Sawyer, Riley Gilbreath, Cole Gore and John-Samuel May. *Photo courtesy of Riley Gilbreath.*

the Bluegrass Heritage Festival in Dallas. A steady stream of performances would soon follow.

Riley Gilbreath and Lone Star Blue have continued to make waves for their blend of traditional bluegrass alongside classic country. They've opened shows for some of bluegrass music's biggest names including Rhonda Vincent and Ricky Skaggs. As of 2022 the group consists of Gilbreath on banjo, Cole Gore on guitar, Sam Smith on mandolin, Leah Sawyer on fiddle and John-Samuel May on bass. This configuration recorded a single, "Dark and Stormy Weather."

Every member of Lone Star Blue has strong bluegrass pedigrees. Prior to teaming up with Riley, both Cole Gore and Sam Smith performed with their respective family bands, Gore in Second Time Around and Sam in Red River Reunion. Leah also performed in her family's band, Simple Gifts, and John-Samuel performed alongside his brother Ethan in the May Brothers.

It's no surprise that Riley Gilbreath has cultivated a successful path in music. One could say that it's in his DNA based on his family lineage. Ultimately his drive, passion and mentorship from the bluegrass community shaped him into the musician he is today. As Jim Penson aptly put it, "If you teach long enough, eventually you'll get a 'Mozart.' Riley is my Mozart!"[11]

Part I

✦

FAMILIES

BANJO BEN AND THE PURPLE HULLS

Yes, we grew purple hull peas, although I can't remember there to actually be a whole lot of back-and-forth contemplation behind naming our band after the crop we grew and loved. Who wouldn't want to name their band after food?
—*Katy Lou Clark*[12]

Traveling 150 miles from Fort Worth to Kilgore is an easy drive on Interstate 20. Though still in Texas, a traveler is leaving the eastern front of the Old West and entering the western edge of the Deep South. The Texas prairies have disappeared in the rearview mirror and the Piney Woods of East Texas lie ahead.

Kilgore is known for its 1930 oil boom, the Kilgore Rangerettes Dance Team and as being the place where one of America's foremost musicians, Van Cliburn, spent his formative years. Harvey Lavan "Van" Cliburn Jr. was born in Shreveport, Louisiana, in 1934. His father, who worked in the oil business, moved the family to Kilgore when Van was six years old.

Van Cliburn's contributions to American music and America–Soviet Union relations are well documented in books such as *Moscow Nights: The Van Cliburn Story—How One Man and His Piano Transformed the Cold War* and *When the World Stopped to Listen: Van Cliburn's Cold War Triumph, and Its Aftermath.*[13] Known as the "Texan Who Conquered Russia," Van would settle in Fort Worth, where the Van Cliburn International Piano Competition has been held since 1962. For decades and generations, Van Cliburn has been an influence on musicians worldwide, including three from his own hometown.

Ben Clark and his twin sisters, Katy Lou and Penny Lea. *Photo courtesy of the Purple Hulls.*

Ben Clark, along with his identical twin sisters, Katy Lou and Penny Lea Clark, were raised on a family farm just outside of Kilgore. The main crop on the farm was purple hull peas (more on that later).

Ben was born in July 1979, and the twins were born in May 1986. Their childhood was unique to say the least. As Ben stated, "I had on one side of the family a lineage of classical music performance and that was mixed with the rural-farmer-ranch lifestyle. I was probably the only kid around practicing Bach pieces and also milking cows before I went to school. I had one foot in the classical music world and the other foot in the cow manure."[14]

Katy Lou added, "Our maternal grandmother [who had been a student of Van Cliburn's mother] was a music educator, and she taught us how to sing harmony and the basics of piano. Our mother plays piano and sings very well. Other than that, we didn't have anyone in the family and didn't know anyone personally who played guitar or any stringed instrument. I think we would've gotten a much earlier start in bluegrass had we been exposed to it earlier and more personally."[15]

Ben further explained how the piano lessons helped him become a multi-instrumentalist:

> *Besides the obvious theory that transfers to every instrument played thereafter, I actually believe the study of piano helped me most with perseverance.*

The piano program I was involved with as a kiddo was quite stringent and structured. Further, my mom knew very well what perfect practice [to achieve perfect playing] *sounded like, and she would accept nothing less. Later on, as I began to play new instruments, what might have discouraged most folks did not discourage me. Yes, I think I had a "knack" for it, but I also put in many hundreds of hours and strategically worked my way through the roadblocks. That instinct and ability to persevere came from my piano studies.*

Katy Lou made the shift to bluegrass in her middle school years. "I first picked up the banjo back in eighth or ninth grade. I didn't have an in-person teacher to begin with, but my brother [Ben] left behind Janet Davis's 'You Can Teach Yourself Bluegrass Banjo' when he was visiting from college, and I started just working through that book on my own. I had been playing piano for several years at that point, so the coordination came pretty quickly."[16]

Penny started her bluegrass exploration on the mandolin. "I was around sixteen years old when I picked up the mandolin. I began by reading notation out of Joe Carr's book 'Texas Fiddle Favorites for Mandolin' and learning the intro to 'Rank Stranger.' I've loved tremolo ever since."[17]

Ben became enamored of the banjo in his late teens:

Interestingly, I wasn't raised in a bluegrass landscape in East Texas. I grew up playing classical piano but wasn't exposed to bluegrass until late high school. There was a festival in a nearby town of Overton. I wasn't drawn to the music initially, I have to admit, but my parents would go and I'd tag along. I remember hearing Chris Jones and the Night Drivers one year and being enamored with his phrasing. I was beginning to play acoustic guitar, and I wanted to play like that. And of course, the banjo is going to catch your attention—whether you like it or not. I do remember being perplexed at how many notes could come out of one instrument. There was a local family band that was really good. They had this young kid on banjo who was the first banjo player I remembered being floored by.

His name was Matt Menefee. He lived nearby in Tyler. He would skateboard between sets and then get up and play the strings off that thing. So, he was another that propelled my interest in the beginning. I was a country music fan but also into classical. As I began to ask around, I found out that my uncle had attempted to play banjo years before. He had this old Fender banjo and a few picks in his closet that he let me have. I had no instruction; there was nothing online like there is now.[18]

Ben did not even know how to put on the banjo picks correctly. He walked up to a banjo picker at a bluegrass festival for advice. He had no idea the musician he was quizzing about banjo picks was the legendary J.D. Crowe.

My first encounter with J.D. was in 1999, I believe. That's when I asked him how to wear banjo picks. Of course, I didn't know who I was talking to back then, and I was mortified to discover the following year that I asked such an elementary question to a banjo legend (with me as a grown man, no less!).

Fast-forward almost a decade to the Stagecoach Festival in Indio, California. Stagecoach was a very eclectic festival with artists from country, pop and even bluegrass. The festival lodged all the artists in the same luxury hotel for the festival. As I walked through the lobby I saw J.D. and his band heading toward me. I just had to ask him, so I stopped him and said, "Mr. Crowe, my name is Ben Clark. I met you at the Overton, Texas, bluegrass festival about a decade ago and asked you…" "You asked me how to wear your picks! I remember you!" He then went on to tell his band members that he couldn't forget it because he'd never had anyone wearing their picks backward come to him for help. We all had a good laugh, at my expense, which was OK. He asked, "What are you doing here in Indio?" I said, "I'm playing banjo for Taylor Swift." He yelled out, "It worked! My advice worked!" We went on to talk another time or two over the years, and he was always so gracious, and we again chuckled about that story.[19]

Ben really fell in love with the banjo during his sophomore year of college at Texas A&M. That's when the nickname "Banjo Ben" started to stick. Ben's banjo mentor was Mitch Key, and Ben credits Mitch for his career in bluegrass:

Mitch Key was my real-life Clayton Delaney. If you know that ol' Tom T. song, you know what I mean, and there's not too much more I can add to the influence Mitch had on me. Mitch was a mess in the best sense of the word, and everyone who met him could never forget him. I couldn't hardly believe a banjo master lived so close to me and that he'd spend such time with me or the fact that he'd accept cigarettes for banjo lesson payment. I miss him, and I wish I could call and tell him what I've been up to and how I wouldn't be pickin' if not for him.[20]

That banjo passion would lead to Ben dropping out of Texas A&M and enrolling in the bluegrass program at South Plains College. In the summer of 2004, Ben led a country band at Six Flags Over Texas in Arlington, Texas. As the calendar rolled to autumn Ben made the move to Nashville. He had an audition to play in Keith Urban's band but did not get the gig. "I was disappointed to finish runner-up but also excited that I almost got such a huge gig after only being in Nashville a short while. I actually learned more in that audition process than I lost by not getting the gig. And looking back, I was not ready. It's clear now that it was a good thing they chose the other guy."[21] By 2006, he was playing piano, mandolin and banjo for recording artist Craig Morgan. In December 2006, Ben's music career would undergo a seismic shift.

Taylor Swift was looking for someone to "do what I do,"[22] as Ben Clark reflected on meeting with Swift in 2006. Ben would join Taylor's touring band that December. The opportunity would lead to touring to huge crowds around the world at venues like London's Wembley Stadium and national television appearances.

One of these television appearances was on *CMT Crossroads*, a collaboration between Taylor Swift and Def Leppard. The meeting between the two bands presented Ben with a teaching opportunity. Ben taught Def Leppard lead singer Joe Elliott "Dueling Banjos" on banjo.

> *Being in Taylor's band meant that we spent a lot of time around fans, artists and celebrities that weren't exposed to country or bluegrass music. We were a pop band, and that's mainly where and what we played. Sometimes I would be a bit nervous to take a banjo into those settings, but it didn't take me long to discover that literally everyone admired the banjo. Sure, there were some jokes here and there, but they weren't serious.*

The Purple Hulls performing. *Photo courtesy of the Purple Hulls.*

I even had R&B and rap artists tell me how cool they thought the banjo was. The banjo allowed me to make friends all over the world, regardless of musical context.[23]

Katy Lou and Penny would follow their brother's path to South Plains College, to play music and to play basketball. Katy Lou recalled,

Five semesters in SPC's music department was absolutely the most formative time in my music journey. My experience there was important and lasting. It's where I learned the basics of so much, really. I knew how to play a few tunes on banjo and piano when I arrived but hadn't a clue how to get off the tab/music or at all how to play with others. I remember not being able to vamp on banjo and sing at the same time. My dad also bought and shipped us our first guitar in college, a Martin D-28. And I remember Alan Munde writing a Nashville number chart on the board the very first day of bluegrass ensemble and having no clue what any of it meant. But I learned. It all made good sense. I soaked it up, and really, I can't believe I had the luxury of attending SPC when I did. I enjoyed every instructor in that department for multiple reasons. Perhaps the most influential in my journey were Alan Munde, Joe Carr and Rusty Hudelson. Alan and Joe's unceasing banter back and forth to one another was like being on the set of a sitcom. I kept a piece of paper in my bluegrass folder on which I would write Munde/Carr quotes. They still give me a laugh![24]

Penny also looked back fondly on her time at South Plains College.

I know that I wouldn't have found myself so diligently into music at that age had it not been for that affordable program and my immersion in it. When I got there, I was so green and intimidated. I had never played much with anyone other than my sister. I was launched into learning how to play in a band and how to play by ear and improvise. It also gave me access to so many old records and CDs, most of which I had never known even existed! Each teacher impacted me greatly, and they all seemed to believe I was more capable than I ever felt I was. Cary Banks was head over the music department there, and his encouragement of me was uplifting and his enjoyment of music inspiring.[25]

Although music won out over basketball, the girls still shoot hoops for fun. In 2009, the lead singer of the country vocal group Rascal Flatts, Gary

LeVox, offered Ben, Penny and Katy Lou a songwriting deal in Nashville. Penny said one of the "dream come true moments" of being a songwriter was sitting down for a writing session with Tom T. and Dixie Hall at their farm in Franklin, Tennessee.

Ben resigned from Taylor Swift's band, and the three siblings began writing, recording and touring as the Purple Hulls. How difficult was the decision to leave Taylor's band?

> *The concerts were small at first, of course, as I started with Taylor as a new artist. The ride thereafter was amazing to watch—something that happens once a generation. She went from new artist to best-selling artist in the world in just two years. That kind of thing doesn't happen often, and I had a front-row seat. It is almost embarrassing how normal the experiences became. In fact, I found myself growing tired of the hustle and desiring some simplicity again. So in that regard, it was in fact not difficult at all to put in my resignation. I'm so very thankful for the opportunities and experiences I had. I know that only a handful of side guys get to see the world from a private jet and giant stage. However, I can honestly say I do not miss it.*[26]

By 2011, Ben had started the first version of his music instruction platform, BanjoBenClark.com. However, 2012 would bring another big change for Ben, Penny and Katy Lou.

In the summer of 2012, Ben, Penny and Katy Lou's father was diagnosed with terminal cancer. The Purple Hull plans were put aside, and Penny and Katy Lou went back to East Texas to care for their father and the farm. Their father passed away a year later.

After a family tragedy it's important to have close friends to confide and spend time with. Katy Lou noted,

> *A memorable experience was Penny and I getting to travel with our dear friends the Quebe Sisters for sixteen months. Five kindred spirits traveling the country and making great music, playing awesome venues and making a lot of people smile. We shouldn't have been allowed to have that much fun. And it was a realized dream playing arch-top guitar in their band and a real challenge for me, as I knew only one closed chord before I started learning their material. No one comes close to doing what they do as well as they do. I was a big fan long before having the opportunity to make music with them. Truly a season in life for which I'm very thankful.*[27]

Two sets of sisters on tour together: the Purple Hulls and the Quebe Sisters. *Photo courtesy of the Purple Hulls.*

The Quebe Sisters are a progressive western swing band from Burleson, Texas. Grace, Sophia and Hulda Quebe made their debut in 2000 at Fort Worth's Red Steagall Cowboy Gathering and Western Swing Festival.

In 2009 the Quebe Sisters appeared on the *Marty Stuart Show* in Nashville, Tennessee. In the same year, backstage at the Grand Ole Opry, the Quebe Sisters met Penny and Katy Lou. The five female musicians soon realized they were fellow Texans and became very close friends, leading to a joint tour in 2014.

Katy Lou went on to elaborate that western swing was a genre the Purple Hulls wanted to explore in more detail: "Oh, yeah! It's on our agenda, for sure. It won't be bona fide western swing, but more like bluegrass infused with Texas swing! The swing influence is showing itself more and more in our live shows and song writing."[28] Penny added, "I'd take some down-home shows with my father-in-law and sister-in-law, swing meisters Dick and Emily Gimble. I married Johnny Gimble's grandson, Jon, and so it would be a family affair!"[29]

In spite of their busy schedules, Ben, Katy Lou and Penny Lea still find the time to perform together. *Photo courtesy of the Purple Hulls.*

Since 2014 Penny and Katy Lou have continued touring and recording as the Purple Hulls. Banjo Ben is still teaching through his website and with his music camps across the country. "I believe a passion for teaching stems from a passion for learning, then a passion for seeing others learn and succeed. That's the reason I started teaching, I wanted others to feel the same exhilaration in learning that new lick. Looking back, I guess I always was drawn to teaching. I often found myself in little training roles in jobs during my teenage years. In grad school, I was able to teach an undergraduate class and lab at Texas A&M. That's the first time I remember thinking: I love watching these people get it. So, I think the passion is a gift I've been given, and it's fueled by igniting the passion in others to improve in their pursuits."[30]

The three musical siblings still get together to play and sing. Katy Lou explains, "The three of us get to make music together on occasion, and that keeps it pretty special, I think. We're not in a time or place that we can all play together full time, so having the opportunity to get together when we do, we're all thankful for. Many times our shows revolve around Banjo Ben's Cabin Camps. That's also a fun time to be able to play music with each other and for other folks."[31]

THE COOKE BROTHERS

On January 22, 2016, the Cooke Brothers band hit the stage at the Allen Texas Bluegrass Festival—seventy-five miles and over sixty years from the July 2, 1949 Navarro County Electric Co-Operative annual meeting and amateur talent contest, where the Cooke Brothers band beat out twelve other competitors, winning twenty-five dollars.[32]

Billy Joe and Wendell Cooke's father was a farmer and a fiddler. The family farm was in Ellis County, between the cities of Waxahachie and Ennis. Like most folks, the family played music for enjoyment, a joyful respite from the hard labor of a family farm. However, with Billy Joe on mandolin and Wendell on guitar, the boys soon found that folks enjoyed listening to their music. The brothers played old-time gospel and country. Then, in late 1945, there was a systematic change in American music. Bill Monroe and the Bluegrass Boys upset the apple cart.

Many rock and pop musicians and music fans point to February 9, 1964, as their musical epiphany. That was the day the Beatles appeared on *The Ed Sullivan Show*. At the time, their appearance set a U.S. television record of 73 million viewers. Two decades earlier, on December 8, 1945, Earl Scruggs and Lester Flatt made their Grand Ole Opry debut as members of Bill Monroe's Bluegrass Boys. Known as the "Original Bluegrass Band," their unique sound has been influencing musicians and cultivating music fans ever since. Two of those musicians were Billy Joe and Wendell Cooke.

In bluegrass, the brothers had found their musical row to hoe. In 1946, the teenage brothers played at the Chautauqua Auditorium in Waxahachie and

A 1964 photo of the Cooke Brothers band. *Photo courtesy of newspapers.com and the* Waxahachie Daily Light.

started playing at rural schools on the weekend. The Cooke Brothers played many shows in the 1940s for Bob Shelton. (Bob, along with his brothers, Joe and Merle, was a Texas-based music act active from the 1930s to the 1960s.)

"Bluegrass music doesn't date back much further than the Cookes," explained Randall Dyess, band member and announcer. "Wendell and Billy Joe are the real deal. They are natural musicians who play for the sake of enjoyment and family."[33] The family musical tradition continued when Larry Cooke, son of Billy Joe, joined the band on banjo.

Larry is not the only musician to get his start with the Cooke Brothers. There have been many others, including the extraordinary fiddler George Giddens. Giddens is known for his "absolutely insane" (according to the folks at the Snuffy Jenkins Festival)[34] version of "Orange Blossom Special." Giddens has been a member of the Dillards since 2019.

Other musicians who cut their teeth with the Cooke Brothers include banjo pickers Scott Vestal, Jeff Scroggins, Don McAfee and Roger Shelton and guitarist Gary Bell.

The Cooke Brothers took a hiatus of around fifteen years to grow their careers, families and businesses. However, by the 1970s and 1980s, the Cooke Brothers were traveling to Arkansas, Louisiana, Mississippi and Oklahoma, never far from their Ellis County homes. The Cooke Brothers band played on shows and festivals with artists such as Vince Gill, Marty Stuart, Ricky Skaggs, Lester Flatt and the Father of Bluegrass, Bill Monroe. The common thread throughout their decades of music making was they did it for fun, not for fame or money. "If ever a dollar was made from our music, we spent it on gas," remembered band member Randall Dyess.[35]

Money to support their families came from their professional careers and businesses. Wendell worked for the Texas Department of Transportation as a highway engineer, while Billy Joe worked in the engineering department of Tyler Refrigeration for nineteen years before starting his own company, C&C Refrigeration, in 1969.[36] Billy Joe's son, Larry Cooke, is also a partner in C&C Refrigeration.

As is the case with any business, stress is a factor that Billy Joe and Larry deal with, especially during the peak season. "Summer is a stressful time," they both agreed. "Customers don't realize they have a problem until after that first heat wave." However, Billy Joe and Larry have found the perfect "stress buster." "We love to play bluegrass and gospel music," Billy Joe

Left: The Cooke Brothers, still pickin' after all these years. *Photo courtesy of the Cooke Brothers.*

Right: Promotional poster for a Cooke Brothers appearance at the Bristol Opry in 2018. *Photo courtesy of the Cooke Brothers.*

A Cooke Brothers promotional photo from 2019. *Photo courtesy of the Cooke Brothers.*

expressed with great enthusiasm. "We've been playing off and on now for some thirty years. It's good, wholesome, family entertainment." The Cooke Brothers band has played in a five-state area, all within driving distance from home, of course. They may take a lengthy hiatus from time to time, but they always return to the music, not only because they love it, but because it beats the stress."[37]

If music keeps you young, there is no greater example than the Cooke Brothers. In their seventh decade of music making, they were playing venues like the Waxahachie Community Theatre, the Bristol Opry, Pearl Bluegrass First Saturday Jam and Stage Show and the Everley Rose Event Center.

The band's last performance was on March 2, 2019, at the Everley Rose Event Center in Waxahachie. According to Billy Joe, the band is now "temporarily retired," but he wouldn't be surprised if they got going again in the future.[38]

For over seventy years, the Cooke Brothers traveled many miles but never too far from their Ellis County home.

Thanks to Sandra McIntosh and Carolyn Willis of Waxahachie Now. *Their articles were an invaluable resource for this story.*

BORN IN TEXAS

native: relating to or describing someone's country or place of birth or someone who was born in a particular country or place[39]

Some folks who were born in Texas moved away at a young age. In cases like this, Texas will claim you as a native Texan—unless you grow up to be a criminal or an embarrassment. Then it's "Oh, they're not from around here"!

For instance, President Dwight D. Eisenhower was born in Denison, Texas, in 1890. Two years later, his family moved to Abilene, Kansas. The Texas Historical Commission has restored the home he was born in, and it is now part of the Eisenhower Birthplace State Historic Site in Denison.

Entertainer/ comedian Carol Burnett was born in San Antonio, but her family moved to Los Angeles when she was six years old. The legendary pop singer Johnny Mathis was born in Gilmer, Texas, and his family moved to San Francisco when he was very young. Trey Anastasio, lead vocalist and guitarist for the jam band Phish, was born in Fort Worth; then his family moved to Princeton, New Jersey, three years later. Buck Owens was born in Sherman, Texas, but after he finished third grade, the family moved to Mesa, Arizona, due to the Dust Bowl and Great Depression.

Comedian and banjo advocate Steve Martin was born in Waco, Texas. His family moved to Garden Grove, California, when he was five. In the world of professional bluegrass Audie Blaylock is another musician born in Texas.

Audie Blaylock was born in El Paso, Texas, in 1962 while his father was stationed at Fort Bliss.[40] Fred Blaylock was stationed at Fort Bliss for two years. After that, the family left El Paso for Lee County, Virginia, where Fred's family was from. Finally, the family settled in Lansing, Michigan. Michigan was the home state of Ruth Blaylock's family, the Hensleys.

Both of Audie's parents played guitar, and his father's brother played banjo. Ruth's father, Noah Hensley, played guitar and also sang. Growing up in a musical family, Audie learned to play guitar and mandolin. He remembers going to bluegrass festivals, Saturday night family jams and falling asleep in a pile of coats. Audie says he thought everyone grew up this way until he was an adult. "I grew up going to bluegrass festivals, and you meet this person and you meet this person and before you know it, you're playing in a band."[41]

Still in his teen years, Audie joined Jimmy Martin's band in 1982.

Well, like I said earlier, I grew up going to bluegrass festivals, and you meet this person and you meet this person. So I kinda met a couple of guys in his band, and we hung out and did some picking. It's just a networking thing; you get introduced. I was playing in a local bluegrass band. We had played in northern Michigan and had gotten home at about four or five o'clock in the morning. Then I got a phone call, probably around seven, and the caller said, "Is this Audie Blaylock? This is Jimmy Martin." And I'm like OK, which one of you yahoos out there is trying to pull some kind of trick. I thought it was someone in the band. He just kept talking; it didn't even slow him down. Then he said something that made me realize that it really was Jimmy Martin, and at that point, he had my full attention. So he said, "I need a mandolin player, do you think you know all the songs? Well, meet me down here on Thursday." So I got a flight to Nashville on that Thursday, and he picked me up, and I spent a couple of weeks at his house. I played in his band for nine years.[42]

After leaving Jimmy Martin, Audie worked with Red Allen until Red's death. Audie also played with Red's son, Harley Allen. Through the 1990s Audie continued working as a sideman, playing mandolin and guitar with the Lynn Morris Band (from Lamesa, Texas) and playing guitar and singing harmony vocals with Rhonda Vincent.

Audie recorded his first solo album, *Trains Are the Only Way I Fly*, in 2001. In the 2000s, he also developed a professional relationship with fiddling ace Michael Cleveland. Audie formed Audie Blaylock and Redline in 2004. As

Audie Blaylock. *Photo courtesy of Audie Blaylock.*

a car enthusiast Blaylock came up with the Redline name for the red line on a vehicle's tachometer. The red line warns a driver that they're pushing it a little too hard.

Between 2009 and 2016, Audie Blaylock and Redline recorded six albums: *Audie Blaylock and Redline*, *Cryin' Heart Blues*, *I'm Going Back to Old Kentucky: A Bill Monroe Celebration*, *Hard Country*, *The Road That Winds* and *Originalist*.

Listening to Audie's albums, you find it's no surprise he grew up listening to his parents' bluegrass and country music records. Imprinted at a young age, he has been strongly influenced by this music, and it shows in his musicianship. When he reached his high school years, he began to listen to the classic southern rock bands such as the Allman Brothers Band, Lynyrd Skynyrd and the Marshall Tucker Band.

He claims the Allman Brothers Band as one of his biggest influences. Not in arrangements or genre but in attitude. "I love the attitude in which they play. I tell my band, yes, we're a bluegrass band, but we can play like a rock-and-roll band. A fiery performance. Hit the stage smoking."[43] Derek Trucks, who played for the Allman Brothers and now leads the Tedeschi Trucks Band with his wife, Susan, remains one of Audie's favorite guitarists. "Derek Trucks, he's not of this planet! As a matter of fact, Reed [Reed Jones, bassist with Audie Blaylock and Redline] and I just saw them again two nights ago in Columbus. It's an eleven-piece band. The cool thing is that Susan took people from her band, and Derek took people from his band and they formed this whole thing so that no one was left behind. It's an incredible, incredible musical experience."[44] Audie also mentioned that working with Derek Trucks would be a dream collaboration. However, Audie's résumé is not lacking when it comes to working with some of the all-time greats.

Audie performing with his band Redline. *Photo courtesy of Audie Blaylock.*

Besides the already mentioned Jimmy Martin, Rhonda Vincent and Michael Cleveland, Audie has been fortunate to jam and callaborate with many famous artists. These include Tony Rice, Doyle Lawson, Ralph Stanley, Del McCoury, Ronnie McCoury, Russel Moore (from Pasadena, Texas) and Jason Carter. One of his most interesting collaborations started with a phone call from Marty Stuart.

Audie had just finished up a tour with Rhonda Vincent when he received a call from Marty Stuart. According to Audie, Marty said something to the effect of "Hey man, I know you just got off the road with Rhonda, but I need to put a band together for Andy Griffith playing at the Grand Ole Opry."[45] Audie answered in the affirmative!

In his youth, Andy Griffith wanted to be a professional singer. But acting was where he made his mark, creating two of television's most iconic characters in Sheriff Andy Taylor and the lawyer Ben Matlock. In the 1990s, Griffith was able to record two gospel albums, winning a 1997 Grammy with the album *I Love to Tell the Story*. At the time of the Grand Ole Opry event, Griffith was collaborating with Marty Stuart on a Christmas album. Audie said the January 18, 2003 Griffith event at the Grand Ole Opry was a once-in-a-lifetime event. Especially for a kid who grew up watching *The Andy Griffith Show*.

In the 2020s, Audie Blaylock and Redline are still going strong, touring, recording and releasing their own coffee brand, Redline Roast: the perfect beverage for a hard-charging, pedal-to-the-metal bluegrass band.

JESSE BROCK (C.W. BROCK FAMILY)

Our genre has exploded with abilities I never expected to see in my lifetime. Technologies have developed so far since my time of learning. Kids are learning faster than ever and lightyears ahead of where I was when I was learning my craft. I grew up in the age of LPs and either lifting the needle or rubbing my finger alongside of a spinning record to figure out stuff.
—*Jesse Brock*[46]

Before beginning a momentous career as a sideman for some of the most prolific acts in bluegrass music and receiving awards for his mandolin prowess, Jesse Brock's journey began humbly by learning and making music with his close-knit family.

Jesse was born on July 18, 1972, in Decatur, Illinois. The sounds of bluegrass would soon become an integral part of his childhood. As Brock recalls, "Music came into my life when I was seven years of age. I had been learning songs with my family and held a microphone before an instrument."[47] A year later, at the age of eight, Brock began playing fiddle with a few introductory lessons from Gaye Harrison.

In 1982, Jesse's father as well as his two sisters, Dawn and Molly, began performing together as C.W. Brock and the Next of Kin. By this time, Dawn was using her mandolin to teach Jesse how to play rhythm and switch between chords. Pretty soon, he would stand on stage alongside the group's hired mandolin player, Steve Aby, a college professor. Eventually, Brock would transition into the mandolin slot permanently during a weekend of

Right: Jesse Brock. *Photo courtesy of Jesse Brock.*

Below: C.W. Brock Family. *From left to right*: Dawn, C.W., Jesse and Molly Jo. *Photo courtesy of newspapers.com.*

performances at Loretta Lynn's Dude Ranch in Hurricane Mills, Tennessee. Jesse recounted that moment in an interview with Daniel Patrick on *The Mandolins and Beer Podcast*:

> *We still had some shows to play that weekend. Later on Saturday, I think he said, "I have to get home and grade papers for Monday," and my dad said, "Well, I don't know what we're gonna do; we really need you for the following day. I guess you gotta get back home to do what you have to do." I found out about it in a meeting afterward and said, "Well, I can do it." My dad said, "Are you sure?" I said, "Yeah." I was pretty confident and fearless back then, and things went fine the next day. That following week my father made the executive decision to let him go and said, "You know, no hard feelings, but this is the beginning of a full family band."*[48]

Shortly thereafter, Brock recorded his first studio album with his family. That summer, the group won the band contest at Bill Monroe's Bluegrass Festival in Bean Blossom, Indiana, which allowed them to make a guest appearance on WSM's *Grand Ole Opry*. Performing with his father and siblings helped Jesse develop his musical skills in numerous ways: "It trained my ear to listen for the dynamics, the swells of energy and how to back up a singer. My father and I were the only soloists in the band, and I had to learn how to be improvisational."[49]

In 1984, two events happened that impacted the Brock Family's musical trajectory. Upon learning of another band called the Next of Kin, the group decided to change their name to the C.W. Brock Family. In November of that year, the family made the move to Trinity, Texas, in their converted RV that started its life as a school bus. As Jesse recalled, "It was professionally painted cream-colored with brown stripes that paralleled the side and angled up and over the top. We even had sheet metal painted brown and riveted down all but three windows in the front. We lived in this when not staying in friends' homes periodically."[50]

The Brocks eventually found an apartment in Conroe, Texas, and would park their bus in the area. Although they only stayed in Texas for two years, the C.W. Brock Family recorded their final album, *Pickin' to Please*, in 1985 at Wise Recording Studios in Conroe. As with most Texas-based bluegrass bands, finding solid work in the area proved to be a great struggle. During this time, the C.W. Brock Family performed primarily at restaurants, local bluegrass societies and festivals in various parts of the United States.

In March 1986, the family flew from Houston to Boston after booking a tour in New England. Not only did they fall in love with the area, but they quickly realized there were greater opportunities for them there musically. This would eventually lead the family to relocate to that region. The C.W. Brock Family would continue to perform together until 1988.

Three years after the family group disbanded, Jesse Brock began the next phase of his musical career as a mandolinist for different artists. In 1992, he joined the Lynn Morris Band. His first outing with the group was a two-week tour in Texas. He remained with Morris until early 1993 but later, in 1998, returned and recorded two albums: *You'll Never Be the Sun* and *Shape of a Tear*. Jesse also performed and recorded as a member of Chris Jones and the Night Drivers, the Dale Ann Bradley Band, Michael Cleveland and Flamekeeper, the Gibson Brothers, Fast Track and Authentic Unlimited, among others.

In 2009 and 2015, Jesse was named Mandolin Player of the Year by the International Bluegrass Music Association.

THE DAVIS BROTHERS
(GREG AND BRAD)

Although Brad Davis is the younger of the two Davis brothers, he actually began playing an instrument before his older brother, Greg. Born on November 15, 1963, Brad started his musical journey playing classical music on a nylon string guitar at age five. Greg, born on May 3, 1962, soon found himself wanting to play music also. He was contemplating the piano until he saw the 1967 film *Bonnie and Clyde*, which ultimately changed his musical trajectory.

The sound of Earl Scruggs's banjo ripping through his iconic tune "Foggy Mountain Breakdown" in the background of Bonnie and Clyde's riveting car chases captivated Greg and many others: "I was going, what in the world is that? What's that sound?"[51]

Another turning point for Greg was when he and his family would tune in to the television show *Hee Haw* every Saturday night. The show, which featured host Roy Clark playing the five-string banjo, elevated Greg's interest in the instrument further. Eventually, he acquired a banjo and began taking lessons with Dick Applegate.

Brad quickly realized that his nylon string guitar couldn't compete volume wise with Greg's five-string banjo, so he asked his parents for a steel-string guitar, which they eventually bought for him.

The brothers began honing their craft by listening to recordings of other artists. Brad found himself studying the guitar styles of Doc Watson and Norman Blake, while Greg found himself enthralled with the three-finger picking of banjo greats such as Alan Munde and J.D. Crowe, among others.

Top: Brad Davis. *Photo courtesy of Brad Davis Music.*

Bottom: Greg Davis performing at Douglas Corner Café in Nashville, Tennessee, 2009. *Photo courtesy of Ted Lehmann.*

Greg recalls, "What Brad and I would do was get LPs and turn a 33⅓ down to 16, and it'll be in a different key, and you were trying to learn those licks. Now we have slow-down mode, apps on your phone and YouTube. It's easier to learn stuff, of course, now."

Another source of inspiration for the brothers was the Shady Grove Ramblers, for whom their father, Bob, played washtub bass in an early incarnation. Greg and Brad would go with their dad to the band's practices and listen to the music in awe. Unbeknownst to both siblings until much later, Bob had been a professional musician at one point, having briefly

Davis & Company's 1983 album *Blue Without You. From left to right*: Greg Davis, Brad Davis, Todd Sinkler and Bob Davis. *Author's collection.*

played piano for country music star Johnny Horton before starting a career as a court stenographer.[52]

Eventually they started playing in jam sessions with other musicians such as Scott and Curtis Vestal, Jon Randall Stewart (known professionally as Jon Randall) and Tammy Rogers. As Greg remembers, "We were all in the same age group. It was really a tight-knight group of young people that you know were just hungry to pick. We had a lot of good players."[53] Another place where the Davis Brothers honed their craft was the Davis Pickin' Parts and Parlor Music Store in Grapevine, Texas, which they owned and operated for several years. Jam sessions would occur there regularly. "That was really fun back then, and every Saturday people would line up in our parking lot. I would get there five or ten minutes before we opened, and there was like ten cars in the parking lot. They were there to pick all day," Greg recalls.[54]

Before long, Greg and Brad started performing in front of audiences. Initially it was just the two of them billing themselves as the Davis Brothers. Eventually, they recruited their father to play electric bass, and they became known as Davis & Company. The group released one studio album, *Blue Without You*, in 1983. Along with Bob, Greg and Brad, Davis & Company included mandolinist Todd Sinkler at that time.

By the time the Davis brothers reached young adulthood, their dream to be professional musicians had been nearly realized. Both siblings made the move to Nashville, Tennessee, toward the end of 1987. Greg soon became employed as a backup musician with the McCarter Sisters, while Brad took a gig with another sister act, the Forrester Sisters.

Brad Davis eventually became a sought-out guitarist, performing and recording with numerous artists, such as Willie Nelson, Marty Stuart, Sam Bush, Earl Scruggs and even film actor Billy Bob Thornton in his band, the Boxmasters.[55] He also was featured on Warren Zevon's final album, *The Wind*, which received the 2004 Grammy award for Contemporary Folk Album. After returning to Texas in 2008, Brad opened his own recording studio, Brick Row Music, where he has recorded several of his own solo projects and has produced other artists. In 2020, he expanded and added a retail store to the studio facility, harkening back to his and Greg's days of managing Davis Pickin' Parts and Parlor.

Brad is well regarded among aspiring guitarists for his instructional materials on the instrument as well as his famous Double Down-Up guitar technique, which he was inspired to create after hearing Eddie Van Halen. He is also an accomplished songwriter, penning songs for artists such as Tim McGraw, Doyle Lawson and Alan Bibey & Grasstowne.

Greg would also go on to a storied career playing and recording alongside artists such as Brooks & Dunn, Emmylou Harris and Sam Bush, among others. Since 2008, Greg has served as the banjoist for bluegrass singer Donna Ulisse.

CHUCK LEE: SANTA MAKES BANJOS

Ovilla, Texas, is the oldest town in northern Ellis County. It's a small town with a population of 4,466 people as of 2022.[56] One of Ovilla's residents is a man who's often referred to by children as Santa Claus, and they would be perfectly valid in saying so. Not only does he look like the jolly man in the big red suit, but also he does have his own workshop. The biggest difference between him and Santa is he builds not toys but rather custom open-back banjos for budding musicians.

Originally, Chuck Lee's primary occupation was working as a plumber. In his spare time, he enjoyed playing the five-string banjo, specifically the old-time clawhammer style that had been popularized by players such as Grandpa Jones and David "Stringbean" Akeman. All of Lee's family played music as a pastime. His journey into building banjos of his own began after growing tired of waiting for a custom banjo he had ordered in 2000.

Chuck Lee with one of his handmade banjos. *Photo courtesy of Chuck Lee.*

Lee soon converted a storage unit into a proper workshop. It was in this building where he completed his first hand-built banjo in April 2002.

Chuck's business as a banjo builder soon grew. His instruments would find their way into the hands of accomplished players such as Béla Fleck, Cathy Fink and Dick Kimmel, among others.[57]

Chuck Lee as Santa Claus. *Photo courtesy of Ivey Photography.*

Several of his children also went on to play music in their own right. His son Nate Lee went on to have a successful career in bluegrass music as a multi-instrumentalist and instrument instructor.[58]

Chuck Lee has also fully embraced his Saint Nick likeness. Since 2011, he and his wife, Tamara (who assists him as Mrs. Claus), have been delighting children in the Dallas–Fort Worth area by spreading the Christmas spirit at various events.[59]

As much as Chuck Lee personifies Santa Claus for children, his skills as a banjo craftsman make a recipient of one of his instruments feel like they've woken up on Christmas morning.

THE PYEATT FAMILY

Tilman Franklin Pyeatt was born on August 26, 1933, in Warm Springs, Arkansas.[60] Much of his early biographical information is unknown. What we do know, however, is that he was a military veteran who served in the air force for over twenty years.

During this period, he met Lena Hisada, a native of Tachikawa, Japan. Born on November 5, 1933, Lena had somewhat of a difficult childhood as she grew up in the postwar Japan reconstruction era. Nonetheless, she would press on and live as fulfilling of a life as possible.[61]

After graduating from high school, Lena went on to become a secretary at the Tachikawa Air Force Base near Tokyo, which is where she first came into contact with Tilman. The couple eventually married in December 1956, and Lena soon gave birth to their first child, Marilyn, in August 1957.

With Tilman's military status, the young family found themselves moving from place to place. Shortly after the couple's oldest son, Gene, was born in April 1960, Tilman was transferred stateside to the air force base in Victorville, California, causing Lena to leave her native Japan and move with her family to the United States.

The Pyeatts, of course, would continue to move from place to place. After two years in Victorville, they relocated to Homestead, Florida, near Miami. While there, Lena gave birth to her and Tilman's youngest son, Lehman, in 1963.

The Pyeatt family's next move would be the small town of Dunlay, Texas, located outside of San Antonio. During this time, Tilman was stationed at the

Lakeland Air Force Base. It's believed that this is where the Pyeatts began their musical pursuits. Tilman—having played fiddle and guitar, among other instruments—had been an accomplished musician for some time. Eventually, his kids learned to play music as well. The oldest, Marilyn, played guitar and bass, while the two sons, Gene and Lehman, would learn banjo and mandolin, respectively. In 1968, the group had a weekly radio show on KMAC in San Antonio. This was the same station where Jimmie Rodgers, known nationally as "the Singing Brakeman," had done weekly radio broadcasts in the 1930s. Although listening audiences wouldn't have known it

THE PYEATT FAMILY
311 PARK STREET, SPRINGDALE, ARK. 72764 PHONE 501/751-5585

The Pyeatt Family circa 1970. *From left to right*: Lehman, Marilyn, Gene and Tilman.

at the time, they were tuning in to hear the first Asian American bluegrass band in Texas.[62]

At the end of Tilman's assignment in Lakeland, the family moved to Springdale, Arkansas. It was there the Pyeatts began making studio recordings. In 1970, the group released a four-song EP, *Where We'll Never Grow Old*, on Rimrock Records. They also recorded a single on the Table Rock label containing "Roll Muddy River" and "You Win Again," although it's unclear when it was released. Both records were issued on 45 RPMs.

In the years to follow, Tilman and Lena would divorce. Tilman would remain in Arkansas, eventually remarrying and becoming a well-respected fiddler within the region. He and his second wife, Molly Pyeatt, released two studio recordings centered on traditional fiddle tunes. Tilman passed away on January 24, 2007, at the age of seventy-three in Prairie Grove, Arkansas.

Two of Lena's children would make their way back to Texas. Marilyn and her husband, Kenny Fry, made their home in North Richland Hills in Tarrant County, while Gene and his wife, Marsha, lived in Trophy Club, a suburb of the Dallas–Fort Worth metroplex. Their mother, Lena, would follow suit in 1995, moving to the Dallas area in order to be close to her children.

Gene was the only sibling in the Pyeatt family who remained musically active. He went on to perform and record with multiple Texas-based bluegrass bands, such as Whitehouse Harmony and Bluefield Express.

Although Marilyn went on to a career working with animals, she never lost her love and passion for music. She passed away on January 18, 2019, at the

 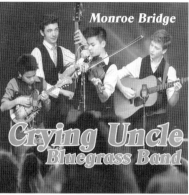

Left: Al Hawkes (*mandolin*) and Alton Myers (*guitar*) were known to radio audiences as Allerton & Alton. They are considered to be the first interracial duo in bluegrass and country music history. *Author's collection*.

Right: Crying Uncle Bluegrass Band's 2020 album *Monroe Bridge*. *From left to right*: Teo Quale, Andrew Osborn, Miles Quale and John Gooding. *Author's collection*.

age of fifty-seven.[63] The family matriarch, Lena, passed away on December 21, 2020, at the age of eighty-seven.

In a musical genre that is predominantly white, the Pyeatt Family certainly blazed a trail. They began performing during a time when other races weren't commonly represented within bluegrass music. While others such as the interracial duo Allerton & Alton had their own radio broadcast in the 1940s and '50s, one could argue that Tilman Pyeatt and his family were one of the earliest examples of a multiracial bluegrass ensemble. In recent times, musicians such as Miles and Teo Quale and Tray Wellington have received recognition for their abilities, proving there's room for everyone in the circle.

THE STEEL DRIVIN' FIDDLER

Before becoming one of the most sought-out backup musicians in Nashville, Tennessee, and cofounding a Grammy-winning bluegrass band that launched the career of country superstar Chris Stapleton, Tammy Rogers's musical journey began in earnest with her family in the Dallas–Fort Worth area.

Tammy was born in Rogersville, Tennessee, on January 18, 1966. When Rogers was five years old, her family left their East Tennessee home and moved to Irving, Texas. Growing up, Tammy was always surrounded by music: "My parents were both musical and actually met at a local radio station. My mom was singing, and my dad was playing in a bluegrass band! I remember them singing around the house from the time I was three or four years old. We always had a few guitars and a mandolin at home."[64]

Tammy's father, T.J., quickly decided that Tammy needed to be musically involved as well: "My dad decided that I should play the violin and signed me up for the school orchestra program when I was ten, in the fifth grade. I fell in love with it almost immediately and never looked back!"[65]

It's unsurprising considering the Rogers's bluegrass background that T.J.'s real motivation for signing young Tammy up for the school's orchestra was to eventually mold her into a fiddler. Pretty quickly, Tammy's dad began teaching her the bluegrass repertoire: "My dad started showing me a few fiddle tunes after I had been playing about three or four months. He could only play by ear, so that's the way I learned them. He would then back me up on the guitar, so I very quickly got used to playing with other people, which

Left: Tammy Rogers. *Photo courtesy of Kevin Smith.*

Right: The Pickin' Tymes studio album *Bluegrass Past – Present – Future. From back to front, left to right*: Wanda Rogers, Tammy Rogers, T.J. Rogers and Scott Vestal. *Author's collection.*

was invaluable."[66] Tammy soon took formal lessons and also continued being part of the orchestra all throughout her years in public school.

Eventually, T.J. taught his wife, Wanda, how to play the upright bass, and the family formed their own band, which became known as the Pickin' Tymes. To complete the group's sound, the Rogers family recruited Kevin Kirkpatrick to play the banjo.

During the period that the Pickin' Tymes performed regularly, the Dallas–Fort Worth metroplex actually had a thriving bluegrass community. As Tammy remembered,

> *It was a great place to grow up as there was already a pretty solid bluegrass scene there. The Southwest Bluegrass Club, if I remember correctly, would sponsor shows at local high schools. There were also lots of festivals in the area during this time period, the late 1970s. I remember the first festival my dad took me to was in McKinney, Texas, and I got to see Keith Whitley with Ralph Stanley and a very young Marty Stuart with Lester Flatt!!! I'll never forget that show. I can still remember it so vividly.[67]*

After Kevin Kirkpatrick departed the band, a fifteen-year-old banjo player named Scott Vestal filled the vacancy. His younger brother Curtis also joined the group on mandolin. This configuration released one studio album, *Bluegrass Past – Present – Future*. Although it's uncertain exactly when the project was released, it is clear that the Pickin' Tymes were a very tight unit with strong vocals from the Rogers family and solid instrumental prowess from the Vestal brothers.

A series of young musicians got their start performing with the Pickin' Tymes. Many went on to have successful music careers in their own right. As Tammy explains, "We were all just a bunch of kids running around to festivals, staying up all night jamming, learning songs and having a ball! It's amazing to me that so many of us went on to professional careers in music. In addition to Scott [Vestal] and Brad [Davis], there was Greg Davis, Billy Joe Foster, Craig Fletcher, Richard Bailey, Russell Moore and a few others."[68]

After Tammy graduated from Nimitz High School in 1983, she attended Southern Methodist University to study classical performance. Rogers soon came to realize that Nashville, known by tourists as Music City, was where her future lay. She went on to finish her college education at Belmont University. From there, Tammy became one of Nashville's sought-after backup musicians, touring with acts such as Patty Loveless, Trisha Yearwood, Emmylou Harris and Buddy Miller.[69]

In 2005, Tammy received a call from former bandmate Mike Henderson, who wanted to see if she would be interested in getting together with some other musicians he knew to play some bluegrass. Rogers recalled that fateful night in an interview with Amy Wright of DittyTV:

> *He* [Mike Henderson] *was the guy that knew all of us. He's the one that called us all together and just kind of casually said, "Hey would you guys like to come over and, you know, jam, play a little bluegrass?" It was a Sunday night, and I said sure; I haven't really played any bluegrass now in about fifteen years, so this could be kind of interesting. I walk in and realize oh Richard* [Bailey]*! I've known him since I was a kid. I'd been hearing* [Chris] *Stapleton's name around town as a songwriter, but I had never heard him sing. The minute he opened his mouth, it was like wow! I just kind of jumped in on harmony, and I would've never thought that my voice would have blended with his like it did. It was just this kind of magical thing.*[70]

That group of musicians consisting of Rogers on fiddle, Chris Stapleton on lead vocals and guitar, Mike Henderson on mandolin, Richard Bailey on banjo and Mike Fleming on bass soon became known to the world as

The SteelDrivers. *From left to right*: Matt Dame, Mike Fleming, Tammy Rogers, Brent Truitt and Richard Bailey. *Photo courtesy of Anthony Scarlatti.*

the SteelDrivers. Three years after their formation, the group released their debut album on Rounder Records, delighting audiences with their unique blend of bluegrass and blues music.

To the group's surprise, the SteelDrivers soared in popularity. Several months before the release of the band's sophomore album, Chris Stapleton departed the band to pursue what eventually became his own successful musical career. A year later, mandolinist Mike Henderson exited as well. As Tammy stated in an interview with John Lawless of *Bluegrass Today* during this time, "Mike had always said that the whole idea was to get together with friends, play some tunes and find a local gig once a month. In his wildest dreams, he didn't think it would grow legs and be as big as this—none of us did."[71]

The SteelDrivers soldiered on, adding acclaimed mandolinist and producer Brent Truitt to the group. Over the years, the band had several different lead singers, including Gary Nichols, Kelvin Damrell and Matt Dame. Nonetheless, the SteelDrivers continued to have critical success, most

Tammy Rogers and Thomm Jutz. *Photo courtesy of Anthony Scarlatti.*

notably receiving the Best Bluegrass Album Grammy award for their 2015 release, *The Muscle Shoals Recordings.*

Even with all of her success as part of the SteelDrivers, Tammy has maintained her own notable career in bluegrass music. In 2021, she released a collaborative album with singer and songwriter Thomm Jutz titled *Surely Will Be Singing* on Mountain Fever Records.

In February 2023, Tammy and the SteelDrivers returned to Texas to kick off their 2023 national tour. At Odessa's Ector Theatre, their opening band was Jade Throneberry with Dawson Marrow and David Barnett. At Buck's Backyard Texas in Buda, Andi Jo Huff and the Hillsiders opened the show.

Jade and Andi Jo continue the tradition of women in Texas bluegrass. You can learn more about Jade and Andi Jo in later chapters of this book.

THE VESTAL BROTHERS
(SCOTT AND CURTIS)

Arlington, Texas, is primarily known for its Major League Baseball team, the Texas Rangers, and for being the founding location of the Six Flags amusement park chain. It's also where bluegrass musicians Scott and Curtis Vestal began their musical journey.

Both of the Vestal brothers were born in Duncan, Oklahoma. The oldest, Scott, was born on May 8, 1962. The youngest, Curtis, arrived on Scott's second birthday in 1964. A few years later, the Vestal family relocated to Arlington.

From an early age, music played an integral role in Scott's and Curtis's lives. The boys were exposed to a wide variety of musical styles, in large part due to their grandfather Famon Self, a fiddler who played in a band that specialized in country, bluegrass and western swing. Pretty soon the brothers began taking part in musical activities themselves. As Curtis recalled, "I can remember playing in Glen Rose at Oakdale Park with Pete and Wimp, who ran that festival, and I think I was on stage around four years old. I think around that time I was just singing and Scott was playing guitar a little bit."[72]

Curtis eventually acquired his own guitar and began playing around the age of six or seven. Not too long after that he started playing the mandolin, which would be his primary instrument for many years.

At the age of thirteen, Scott started learning the five-string banjo, the instrument that he ultimately became known for. The brothers had a wide range of musical influences as they were honing their respective crafts. For Scott, it was banjoists such as Earl Scruggs and Little Roy Lewis and

Texas-based musicians Gerald Jones and Eddie Shelton. For Curtis, it was mandolinists such as Dempsey Young, Buck White and Ricky Skaggs. While discussing his inspirations Scott commented, "I was equally influenced by bands, not just individual musicians. The whole band working together always made me feel excited about music."[73]

Pretty soon, Scott and Curtis began playing in different Texas-based bands together such as Pickin' Tymes and Davis & Company. At age eighteen, Scott got his first big break on the national bluegrass scene as the banjoist for Larry Sparks & the Lonesome Ramblers. He appeared on Sparks's 1981 release, *Ramblin' Letters*.

A year later, Scott departed the Lonesome Ramblers to form the group Southern Connection with eighteen-year-old vocalist Russell Moore. This band musically reunited the Vestal brothers, as the original lineup included Scott on banjo, Curtis on mandolin and Moore on guitar. The group also had a few different bassists, including Russell's brother Steven, who played on Southern Connection's only studio release in 1984. For a brief period of time, Curtis left the band. He would eventually return to Southern Connection, but not as a mandolinist. "Scott called me and said, 'Hey, you wanna get back in the band?' I'm like sure. He said, 'Well, you'll have to play bass.' I'd never even played a bass; I'd never even listened to bass players really. So we found an old bass, and I started learning to play."[74]

Shortly after Curtis rejoined the group, Southern Connection opened a show for Doyle Lawson & Quicksilver in Tarkington, Texas. Impressed by what he heard, Lawson kept them in the back of his mind. In 1985, the band made a joint decision to move to North Carolina together. Before they even had the opportunity to propel their career further, Doyle called asking if Scott, Curtis and Russell would be interested in becoming members of Quicksilver. Although it would mean the end of Southern Connection, the three men jumped at the chance.

During this period of Scott's and Curtis's careers, both men got an intense musical education. The first six weeks of their tenure with Lawson involved rigorous rehearsals that often lasted eight to ten hours a day. The new configuration of Quicksilver soon started touring and released the gospel album *Beyond the Shadows* in 1986.

Following the project's release, Curtis left Doyle Lawson & Quicksilver and moved back home to Arlington. Scott remained a member of the band for the next two years, appearing on a total of five albums with Quicksilver.

After Scott departed Doyle Lawson & Quicksilver, he went on to perform with numerous configurations, such as Livewire, Continental Divide and

Above: Doyle Lawson & Quicksilver, circa 1985. *From left to right*: Curtis Vestal, Doyle Lawson, Russell Moore and Scott Vestal. *Photo courtesy of Jim McGuire.*

Left: Scott Vestal. *Courtesy of Pinecastle Records.*

the Sam Bush Band, among others. Most notably, he spent the year 2006 recording and touring with rock singer David Lee Roth.[75]

He also began a storied career in audio engineering and production. As Scott explains, "I've been into recording music as long as I've been playing. I was always fascinated with it. Over the years, I have collected microphones and preamps and have built several studios in Georgia, and Tennessee. In 1999, I built my studio Digital Underground just outside of Nashville, Tennessee, that I work out of to this day, producing and recording bands and solo artists and playing on tracks that people send to me."[76] Scott has produced and appeared on recordings with countless artists among the likes of Bill Monroe, Dolly Parton and Donny and Marie Osmond.

Scott has received several awards for his prowess as a banjoist. The International Bluegrass Music Association named him Banjo Player of the Year in 1996 and again in 2020. In 2017, he received the Steve Martin Prize for Excellence in Banjo and Bluegrass.

Although the Vestal brothers occasionally reunited for different musical outings such as Scott's 1992 solo recording, *In Pursuit of Happiness*, and Doyle Lawson's twenty-fifth-anniversary reunion concert in 2004, Curtis remained in Texas working in various

Curtis Vestal. *Photo courtesy of Curtis Vestal.*

industries, such as manufacturing, auto sales and power sports. In 2018, Curtis sold his home and made the move to Gallatin, Tennessee, near Nashville to return to the music business: "I had kinda been yearning to get back into it. People would send me messages about how they loved my playing, and I'm like, 'You're just twenty years old, how do you even know? You weren't alive when I was playing.' I just kind of felt called from a higher power."[77]

Following Curtis's reentry into music, he made several appearances with both Jesse McReynolds and Bobby Osborne on WSM's *Grand Ole Opry*. He has also performed and recorded with Steve Thomas & the Time Machine, Dale Ann Bradley and Tina Adair and Darren Beachley, among others. He and Scott would also appear together on the all-star instrumental recording *Bluegrass 2020*, which was nominated for Album of the Year by the International Bluegrass Music Association in 2021. In 2022, Curtis released the single "Cabin on the Hill," his first recording under his own name. The following year, Vestal released his second single, "Time."

THE WHITES

In 2015, virtuoso guitarist Ry Cooder was watching a YouTube video of Ricky Skaggs performing with the Whites. The Whites are a family band consisting of Ricky's wife, Sharon; sister, Cheryl; and father, Buck. Cooder, who has collaborated with Taj Mahal, the Buena Vista Social Club, Rosanne Cash, the Chieftains, the Rolling Stones and many others, reached out to Ricky and Sharon about a potential tour.

The Cooder, Skaggs and White ensemble rehearsed for a year in Nashville before heading out on the road. Cooder could not contain his excitement for the collaboration. "I've heard all the mandolin players. I'm gonna tell you right now, I don't care who you say, this is the best. He plays some dog s—— up there that is just amazing." And he calls Buck White "as deep a character as I've ever met....He's a source guy. He's the best."[78] Buck White is the patriarch of the White family.

H.S. White was born in rural Oklahoma on December 13, 1930. He changed his name to Buck because of his hero, cowboy movie star Buck Jones. Instead of acting, though, Buck pursued music and became proficient on banjo, fiddle, guitar, harmonica, mandolin and piano. His family moved to Wichita Falls, Texas, where Buck would spend much of his youth.

Buck, like most folks from his generation, grew up listening to music on the radio. He learned harmony listening to the Delmore Brothers, the Monroe Brothers, the Stamps Quartet from Dallas and the Stamps Ozark Quartet from Wichita Falls. Buck stated, "Harmony is the key to good bluegrass music."[79]

Buck White and Down Home Folks, Kerrville Bluegrass Festival, Texas, September 2, 1977. *From left to right*: Doc Hamilton, Bob Black, Buck White, Sharon White and Cheryl White. *Photo courtesy of Rick Gardner.*

While still in high school, Buck met fiddler Arnold Johnson. Arnold and Buck formed a four-piece band. The band members started out rough around the edges, but the determined beginners became a polished band with paid gigs. Buck's father wanted him to attend college, but the music bug had already bitten.

Buck heard about an audition at KRBC radio in Abilene. KRBC was looking to hire a band to back a country music singer on a Saturday night show, *Hillbilly Circus*. Buck's band got the gig and were given a daily show at 11:30 a.m. in addition to the Saturday night show. The band added a couple of members and called themselves the Blue Sage Boys.[80]

Due to sponsor changes, the Blue Sage Boys were out of business after their first year. Buck joined a dance band that traveled around Abilene but eventually moved back to Wichita Falls.

In the early 1950s Buck partnered with Radio King Bill Mack of KWFT and played piano for anyone who needed a piano player, including the Nat Fleming television show. Buck was also playing dances around Wichita Falls. In 1951, Buck married Pat Goza. Two daughters soon followed: Sharon (born on December 17, 1953) and Cheryl (born on January 27, 1955). The Whites would have two more daughters, Rosie and Melissa.

Buck's proficiency on the piano led him to being a sideman for Grand Ole Opry stars, playing in Wichita Falls. During this time Buck backed Ernest Tubb, Lefty Frizzell, Hank Locklin, Webb Pierce, Hank Snow and many others. Buck also played with Bob Wills and the Texas Playboys when they rolled through Wichita Falls.[81] Buck also played the Cowtown Hoedown in Fort Worth with his band the Black Mountain Boys.

In the early sixties Buck was working during the day and playing nightclubs at night to make ends meet. With a growing family, Buck resigned himself to the fact that he was going to be a full-time father and provider, playing music when he could.

Buck moved his family to Arkansas and acquired a steady job. During this time, White performed occasionally, including on local radio programs and television shows. White's wife and daughters joined him to form a band during this period.[82]

The band Buck White and the Down Home Folks, featured Buck on mandolin and vocals, Sharon on guitar and vocals, Cheryl on bass and vocals and Mother Pat on vocals. The band began to travel the bluegrass circuit. They would record four albums: *Buck White & the Down Home Folks*, *In Person*, *That Down Home Feeling* and *Poor Folks' Pleasure*.

Buck White and the Downhomers on the cover of the May 1973 edition of *Bluegrass Unlimited. Author's collection.*

"In 1975, they played a gig with another country star who was about to break through. They made such an impression on Emmylou Harris that she recruited Sharon and Cheryl to record background vocals on her 1978 album *Blue Kentucky Girl*, and took The Whites on the road with her. Sharon fell in love with Emmylou's bandleader, a young bluegrass singer and picker named Ricky Skaggs."[83]

For the Emmylou Harris tour Buck and the Down Home Folks would simplify their name to "The Whites." The exposure and recognition of opening for Emmylou would lead to a recording contract.

The Whites released five top-ten singles on the country music charts between 1982 and 1984: "You Put the Blue in Me," "Hangin' Around,"

The Whites album *Forever You. Author's collection.*

"I Wonder Who's Holding My Baby Tonight," "Give Me Back That Old Familiar Feeling" and "Pins and Needles." They were also inducted into the Grand Ole Opry in 1984.

Playing bluegrass festivals across the country allowed the White family to meet many other bluegrass artists. In 1971, Sharon met Ricky Skaggs and developed a longtime friendship. That friendship led to their marriage in 1981.

A track that has a special place in the Skaggses' hearts is Townes Van Zandt's "If I Needed You," which Sharon says takes them back to August 4, 1981—when they sang the song to each other on their wedding day. "Our pastor said, 'What if you did your unity candle symbol in songs rather than candles? He sings one to you, you to him, and you sing together.' We liked that idea, and this was the one we sang together. We had no idea how hard it

The Whites album *Whole New World. Author's collection.*

was going to be to do. We were both very emotional."[84]

Sharon and Ricky had a top-ten country hit with "Love Can't Get Any Better Than This." The couple also recorded the album *Hearts Like Ours* in 2014. Ricky also collaborated with his in-laws on numerous projects including the albums *Salt of the Earth* and *A Skaggs Family Christmas*, volumes 1 and 2.

Buck also continued his music throughout the eighties and into the new millennium. Buck played mandolin and piano on the Jerry Douglas album *Everything Is Gonna Workout Fine*. He also recorded with the Nitty Gritty Dirt Band on their second volume of *Will the Circle Be Unbroken*.

He appeared in the Greatest Hits collections by Kathy Mattea and Mark O'Connor. Buck's original song "Down Home Waltz" was included on the album *Bluegrass Mandolin Extravaganza*. The album included songs performed by Sam Bush, David Grisman, Jesse McReynolds, Frank Wakefield, Del McCoury on guitar and Buck's son-in-law, Ricky Skaggs. The album received two International Bluegrass Music Association awards in 2000 for Instrumental Recorded Performance of the Year and Collaborative Recording of the Year.

Buck continued to collaborate and appear on multiple recordings, including *Americana Music Series: Bluegrass, Bluegrass Spirit: Twelve Songs of Faith, Gloryland—30 Bluegrass Gospel Classics, How Great Thou Art: Gospel Favorites from the Grand Ole Opry*, Ken Kolodner's *Journey to the Heartland* and Hunter Berry's *Wow Baby!*.

In 2002, The Whites lost the matriarch of the family when Pat died of a heart attack. However, the family music tradition carries on through two of Buck White's grandchildren, Mollie and Luke Skaggs. Both Molly and Luke lean toward contemporary Christian music. Molly released her debut album, *Overtaken*, in 2017. Luke was a coproducer on the album. Luke also played violin, banjo, guitar and viola on other artists' albums, including the Lowland Hum album *Native Air*.

Part II

━━≫≫≫≪≪≪━━

MENTORS

A DAWG AND A HERD OF LONGHORNS

On July 4, 1987, David "Dawg" Grisman took the stage at the Nacogdoches Bluegrass Festival in Nacogdoches, Texas. The festival was a star-studded affair that included Tony Rice, Norman Blake, Jerry Douglas, Byron Berline, Country Gazette, Hickory Hill, the Nashville Bluegrass Band and Mark O'Conner.

David Grisman is probably the most prolific mandolin picker in the long history of American music. Born in Hackensack, New Jersey, in 1945, he has recorded over fifty albums as a bandleader or coleader. His collaborations read like a who's who of music. In the early 1960s, he played with the Even Dozen Jug Band, which also included Maria Muldaur, Stefan Grossman and John Sebastian. At the age of seventeen, Doc Watson invited him to sit in on Doc's rendition of "In the Pines."

Before leaving for California, in 1970, he also played in Red Allen's bluegrass band, the Kentuckians, and was a member of the psychedelic fusion band Earth Opera (which also featured Peter Rowan).

After moving to California, he began to collaborate with Tony Rice and Jerry Garcia. A jam session between Rice, Garcia and Grisman led to the famous *Pizza Tapes* album. Garcia and Grisman were also members of the bluegrass band Old and in the Way, which included Peter Rowan, fiddler extraordinaire Vassar Clements and bassist John Kahn. Grisman and Garcia went on to record six albums together. Grisman and Tony Rice recorded the album *Tone Poems*, and Rice played guitar in Grisman's David Grisman Quintet.

David Grisman performing in Nacogdoches, Texas, July 4, 1987. *Photo courtesy of Rick Gardner.*

Grisman would also develop a bond with Stéphane Grappelli, violinist in Django Reinhardt's Quintette du Hot Club de France. His other collaborations have included a wide range of artists, including Sam Bush, Danny Barnes, Del McCoury, Andy Statman, Beppe Gambetta and Martin Taylor.

Who could have known decades after Grisman's performance in Nacogdoches that his musical influence would be felt on the University of Texas campus? However, before we travel to the home of the Texas Longhorns our story makes a side trip to California and Stanford University.

Richard Somers grew up in Palo Alto, California. His mother loved music, and his father was a captain for Pan American Airways. On one of his international travels, his father purchased Richard a guitar in Japan. Richard became a fan of Mississippi John Hurt and spent years learning finger picking on guitar.

Richard first met David Grisman after a Grisman–Vassar Clements set on Stanford University's KZOO radio station. About a week later, he ran into Grisman at a local music store and asked Grisman if he would give him mandolin lessons. As the lessons progressed, Grisman asked David to compose a tune and bring it to his next lesson.

The tune Richard composed was "Ricochet." "Ricochet" was such a great tune it appeared on the first David Grisman Quintet album in 1977. "Ricochet" has become a beloved standard to mandolin pickers and fans.

David Grisman with "Slade" (Charles Sawtelle) performing in Nacogdoches, Texas, July 4, 1987. Charles Sawtelle was a phenomenal guitar player born in Austin, Texas, but raised in Colorado. Charles was most known as the guitarist for Hot Rize. His Slade character was part of the band's alter ego, Red Knuckles and the Trailblazers. Charles passed away from leukemia in 1999. *Photo courtesy of Rick Gardner.*

Matthew Lyons. *Photo courtesy of Burnt Orange Bluegrass.*

Richard moved to Austin in 1992. He continued his mandolin studies with Paul Glasse. Paul Glasse played a five-string electric mandolin in the University of Texas Jazz Orchestra. Glasse is also a former National Mandolin Champion. He has performed and recorded with artists such as Willie Nelson, Lyle Lovett, Joe Ely, Allison Krauss and Jerry Douglas. Richard would also join the Austin Mandolin Orchestra and start teaching mandolin students himself. One was a young man from Richardson, Texas, Matthew Lyons, who did a short write-up on his experience becoming a mandolin player:

Coming to the University of Texas at Austin (UT) as a freshman was an intimidating process. It was my first time living in a new city other than my hometown of Richardson, Texas. I did not have many friends, and even fewer that I counted as close to me. But through bluegrass music, I would come to make many friends. I would even build up my own formal community around me called Burnt Orange Bluegrass. But at the start, I only had one true friend. He was a friend from high school named Alex Sobotka. And he played the banjo.

Before coming to UT, I had gotten a guitar my final Christmas season in high school. I played occasionally, but did not practice regularly or consider myself competent by any standard. Alex on the other hand, was more polished on his respective instrument than I was on mine. Looking back, I would rate his banjo skills as those of an experienced beginner; he was well practiced but unfamiliar with much of the bluegrass banjo language. Being friends, Alex and I occasionally played music together in high school once I received my guitar. We continued this activity after our arrival at UT together. Our occasional jam sessions were fun, and offered solace in a courtyard or dorm room when the university's pressures seemed too much. Since neither of us knew any formal songs, our time during these meet ups were mostly spent trying to write our own songs. For those curious, we did manage to create one song after many uncounted jam sessions. However, our most eventful musical journey together happened on Saturday, September 24, 2014, only a month after arriving on UT's campus.

The backstory to how I had heard about the concert on this fateful night is sadly uneventful. I had listened to Celtic song sometime in high school and started a Pandora radio station on the topic. On that radio station, the music of Chris Thile happened to come on. After the September concert, I would come to find out that Chris Thile was considered to be one of the best mandolinists of all time, if not the best. But at the time, I simply thought that Chris Thile's music sounded pleasant. I especially appreciated the silky pop that his mandolin pick made when it plucked the mandolin strings. The songs I listened to at the time were "Big Sam Thompson" and "Song for a Young Queen." After listening to these songs for some time in my high school career, I recognized his name when seeing an advertisement for the Bass Concert Hall on UT's campus. He was going to be playing a duet concert with bassist Edgar Meyer at the end of September. I grabbed two tickets in early August that year and quickly invited the closest friend who I knew would be in town with me.

Alex and I arrived at the concert early and sat down in our seats near the front of the concert hall, smiling uncontrollably. Two gentlemen sat to my right and Alex on my left. New to the university, and still overeager to introduce myself to people, I struck up conversation with the gentlemen to my right. I came to find out that one them was a former professional mandolin player named Richard Somers. The other was the director of the Austin Mandolin Orchestra, Joel Hobbs. I would eventually become a student to both of them. After finding out that they both played mandolin, I expressed my own interest in the instrument, stating my own appreciation for its tonal quality. They smiled and continued our conversation, giving me encouragements. They went so far as to even give me advice on how to get my own mandolin. There was a shop on Thirty-Eighth Street that specialized in selling mandolins among other acoustic instruments in traditional music. They continued to give me more advice, but the concert was about to begin. Needless to say, the music was phenomenal. In fact, I was so impressed, that the following Friday, I found myself at Fiddler's Green, the mandolin shop on Thirty-Eighth Street.

My friend Alex helped me pick out the mandolin that I liked. It was a used Washburn mandolin from the 1980s. A mandolinist named Jethro Burns had his signature imprinted on the tailpiece of this model. However, it was at the top end of my budget. Hesitating to make such a big purchase, I asked the shop to hold the instrument overnight so I could sleep on the decision. The next day was my birthday. I had called my parents that evening and told them about the purchase I was contemplating. My mother, because of the timing of the purchase, said she could help pay for half of the instrument. When I woke up the next morning I called Fiddler's Green to let them know I would be purchasing the 1980s Washburn mandolin.

Alex and I showed up at the shop that Saturday afternoon. The mandolin was sitting under the counter when we arrived. After talking to the attendant about necessary accessories for the instrument, such as picks and straps, I was all set. The purchase was rung up and the card was swiped. As I finished my signature, the door chimed and a man walked into the quaint shop. It was Richard Somers. I excitedly waved hello and showed him my new mandolin, thanking him for his advice. I vividly remember the smile that he gave me after my exclamations. He offered his congratulations and followed up by asking if I had a teacher. After telling him that I did not have any lesson teacher, he offered to teach me private lessons on the instrument. I said yes, and my journey with the mandolin had begun.

Up until this point I have not mentioned much in terms of bluegrass. However, that is because I didn't know what bluegrass was at the time. It wasn't until my first lesson with Richard that I figured out that the mandolin was mostly used in bluegrass music. Even though the music was slightly new to me, for I had grown up listening to Today's Country, I was too excited with my new instrument to care about what that meant. My mandolin might as well have been strapped to my torso with duct tape. I took that instrument everywhere and would play it for the few friends I had made on campus so far. So much was my excitement that it came up in every conversation I had for a several months. Eventually, this habit led me to be introduced to a banjo player named James Smith. We played one jam together before parting our separate ways, expecting not to see each other outside of the one event we had set up. Later, I would form a band with him and even attend his wedding.

Skipping to my second semester at UT, I was still taking lessons with Richard. At this point, I had also joined the Austin Mandolin Orchestra and put myself under the conductorship of Joel Hobbs, the other man who had been at the Chris Thile and Edgar Meyer concert. But on the other side of my music social life, I no longer spent much time with Alex. As what happens with some friends, we gradually grew farther apart because we no longer shared classes together. Eventually, we would only share lunch occasionally and play music together on the rarest occasions. Essentially without a friend to play music with anymore, I did most of my mandolin playing at night, outside my dorm, facing the street on a stone table where I wouldn't disturb my roommate. It was on one of these nights that a fellow student named James Tabor walked by and saw me playing my mandolin. He stopped to talk and expressed his interest in my mandolin. He asked if I liked bluegrass music. At this point, I had been playing the music for a little while and nodded to him that I did. He followed up by saying he played the banjo and enjoyed bluegrass music as well. He invited me to a jam session that he and two other banjo players held on Friday afternoons. I hurriedly replied that I would be there and James Tabor continued on his way. This conversation started what would lead me to help found the organization on UT's campus called Burnt Orange Bluegrass.

The jam session was located in front of the Student Activity Center (SAC). I showed up the following Friday early. I had invited Alex, but he couldn't come; so I sat alone, tuning my instrument and waiting. Soon, a student walked up holding a banjo case. He had on a straw hat and was dressed in slacks and a dress shirt. His name was Adrien Lavergne. He was a French graduate student who had recently picked up banjo. Sometime later, another banjo player showed up. It was James Smith. I smiled at the familiar face, and we reminisced of our evening spent together in the past semester. Lastly, James Tabor arrived. After a few more pleasantries, we all pulled out our instruments, tuned, and started the jam.

Similar to my times with Alex, we didn't know many songs, so we would make up our own. However, we did not belabor the details as much as Alex and I did, and we enjoyed the racket that we made. James S. was actually a competent musician compared to the rest of us in attendance, so occasionally, he would lead us in a song he knew. We had fun and enjoyed our time spent in the Friday afternoon sun. A phrase I picked up from James Tabor

The Burnt Orange
Bluegrass Band in 2015.
*Photo courtesy of Burnt
Orange Bluegrass.*

*was "Come for the pickin', stay for the grinnin'." I jammed with them two more times that
semester before it was time for summer, and we went back to our respective homes.*

*The next fall, the jam session started up again. Our Friday escapades continued. Other
musicians would occasionally join us because we were so visible on campus. However, I
wanted a little more, so I sought out an extra jam session in the city lead by the Central
Texas Bluegrass Association (CTBA). Richard, my lesson teacher, had suggested the jam
session to me. My first jam session was on a hot August afternoon in 2015 with about
fifteen people picking away at their various instruments. I had an amazing time, and
although I was still a beginner, I was welcomed by the older members of the circle. Upon
returning to the CTBA jam a second time, I came upon another mandolin player by the
name of Sol Chase. Upon asking, I discovered he was an accomplished veteran of the
mandolin and had just started at UT–Austin as a freshman. Upon hearing his status as a
student, I quickly invited him to the jam session that we held on Friday afternoons. He was
excited as well, and we swapped phone numbers before parting ways that day.*

*Sol showed up at the next Friday jam session. He knew many songs and would lead us
in many of the songs that we played. Between him and James S., the Friday jam sessions
began to take on new life. Soon we got the notion to make our jam session group an official
organization of the UT campus. Adrien suggested the name Burnt Orange Bluegrass. After
paying our fees, we were established. Almost three years later, and with many stories garnered
since, that jam group is still on campus with many new faces smiling and picking away.[85]*

Burnt Orange Bluegrass is a registered student organization, and all
members must be University of Texas students. Every Friday afternoon
the organization hosts a weekly jam by the Martin Luther King statue on
campus. The jams are open to any player.

One Burnt Orange Bluegrass member is Amy Rester, who graduated from the University of Texas in 2022:

> *In fact, we have a reputation for "loudly inviting" instrumentalists who happen to walk by during our jams to join us. Most of our members have no bluegrass experience prior to joining. We teach bluegrass beginners the bluegrass basics like chopping [and] harmonized singing and the bluegrass standards. We like to call ourselves "the most low-stress org you can be a part of." I like to call us a "bluegrass incubator." We have higher standards for players who perform with us, but our open jams are very relaxed.[86]*

Amy, from Rockwell, Texas, began violin lessons at the age of five. Classically trained, Amy was a part of her public school orchestra program, the Texas Music Educators Association All-Region Orchestra, the New Conservatory Dallas and the Greater Dallas Youth Orchestras. As a teenager Amy studied with Ron Neal of Dallas and Julia Bushkova, professor of violin at UNT College of Music, and was a member of the Rockwall Philharmonic Orchestra Board and the Dallas Symphony Orchestra Teen Council.

Amy was also exposed to bluegrass and other genres of folk music at a young age. Amy shared those experiences:

> *Although classically trained, I gravitated toward bluegrass and its subgenres from a young age as well. I remember singing gospel songs at church and going to small, local fiddle camps as an elementary student. I convinced my violin teacher at the time to let me learn fiddle tunes instead of etudes (I traded Wohlfahrt for Mike Weeg's Violinist's Guide to Fiddling). I vacationed to Mountain View, AR, the summers after my fifth and sixth grade years where I tried true picking for the first time. After my second pilgrimage, I set aside bluegrass for almost ten years to focus on my other love, classical violin.[87]*

Her plans to audition for music schools were derailed when she developed a violin-related nerve compression injury. The injury led her to the University of Texas–Austin's McCombs School of Business. However, Amy remained involved in music. She played with the University of Texas Lab Orchestra, Volunteer Chamber Orchestra and the University Orchestra.

Amy's path back to bluegrass occurred in the spring of 2021. "I met a legend of Burnt Orange Bluegrass named Sammy Sanchez (guitar, vocals). He asked me nine times to come to BOB's open jams that semester (we

Top: The Burnt Orange Bluegrass Band performing at a Round Rock Express game in 2018. *Photo courtesy of Burnt Orange Bluegrass.*

Middle: Amy Rester, Burnt Orange Bluegrass and University of Texas alum, graduating in 2022. *Photo courtesy of Amy Rester.*

Bottom: The Burnt Orange Bluegrass Band logo. *Photo courtesy of Burnt Orange Bluegrass.*

later counted). I attended none due to schedule restraints. It wasn't until that summer I was able to get involved. Because bluegrass was a completely new style to me, I was nervous and unconfident. But I stuck with it and laughed at my mistakes and got better." Amy is just one of the many members of Burnt Orange Bluegrass who started as a mentee and became a mentor.

Burnt Orange Bluegrass has become an in-demand ensemble for festivals and events around the Austin area. They have performed for KOKE FM, Austin's Trail of Lights, the Cactus Café, the Jester King Brewery, Bevo Blvd (pregame performances for the University of Texas Longhorn football team), BD Riley's, the Hole in the Wall, the Forty Acres Fest, Texas Revue and the Texas Athletics Games.

Burnt Orange Bluegrass alumni have also gone on to professional careers. Matthew Lyons plays mandolin for the Houston-based Space City Nomads. Mandolin picker Sol Chase and fiddler John Thomas, both based in Austin, are playing professionally.

Amy Rester also gives credit to the Austin bluegrass scene for their support of Burnt Orange Bluegrass:

> *Everyone has been very supportive and welcoming. It's a great community to be a part of. Professional musicians invite Burnt Orange Bluegrass to play at their residencies and invite us to jams they host at their houses. David "McD" McDonald (guitar, vocals) gave us a coaching session to help us play more authentic grass and "gel" together as a band. Phil Brush (bass, vocals) invited us several times to play at his residency at Jester King Brewery. Eddie Collins (banjo) of CTBA invited us to play at the open mic nights he coordinates at New World Deli in Austin. Everett Wren let me share the stage with him and then invited me and my band members to his monthly Butterfly Bar Bluegrass jams. We really appreciate the support from all the Austin grassers and the greater Austin community.*[88]

Burnt Orange Bluegrass leaves an open call for interested students: "We're a group of bluegrass lovers and musicians. We show up for the pickin' and stay for the grinnin'. Join us for our weekly jam sessions 4:00 p.m. on Fridays near the SAC! Musicians of all skill levels welcome!"

Contact Information

E: burntorangebluegrass@gmail.com

CAMP BLUEGRASS
AT SOUTH PLAINS COLLEGE

I might be slightly biased but it's the best camp I've ever been to.
When I was a student, the teachers were so helpful and nice, and the learning
environment was always pleasant and creative! The last two camps,
I have instructed, but the good vibes are still the same!
—multi-instrumentalist Jade Throneberry (fiddle, bass, mandolin, guitar)[89]

Approximately halfway between Lubbock, Texas, and the New Mexico state line stands South Plains College. The community college is located in Levelland just off State Highway 114. South Plains College has a significant legacy in bluegrass music. The school started associate degrees in country music and bluegrass in 1976.[90] "Between classes, there were jams. Everywhere you look, someone was pickin' under a tree, in a hallway or a dorm room. Teachers would jam with students and remembered everybody's name. Positivity was encouraged; it was a totally connected, shared passion," notes Lonnie Joe Howell, speaking about the music program at South Plains College.[91]

The music program at South Plains College is like a tree; the roots have grown deep over the years, branches have spread out and seeds have been spread. Vocalist Lee Ann Womack, Ron Block of Alison Krauss and Union Station, Natalie Mains of the Chicks and Jeremy Garrett of the Infamous Stringdusters attended South Plains College.

Another seedling that sprouted from the South Plains College music program is Camp Bluegrass. John Hartin, chairman of the South Plains

Photography by
Timothy W. Burnett

Jade Throneberry. *Photo courtesy of Jade Throneberry.*

College Creative Arts Program, had the idea of adding a multiday summer workshop. Hartman handed the idea over to banjo virtuoso Alan Munde, multi-instrumentalist Joe Carr and his wife, Paula Carr, to brainstorm and refine the Camp Bluegrass concept. Alan Munde (1986) and Joe Carr (1984) were instructors at South Plains College. "Alan and Joe had the music side covered, but they were not administrative people. That's where I came in," said Paula Carr.[92]

The inaugural summer workshop was held in 1987. The instructors were led by Joe Carr and Alan Munde along with members of his band, Country Gazette. "In the first year, I think they had maybe fifteen students, but the next year, it got bigger," remembered Carr.[93] The camp is held annually for one week in July.

Joe Carr, a master of mandolin, guitar, banjo and ukulele, passed away in 2014. Paula Carr, Joe's widow, and Alan Munde continued to run the camp as codirectors.

Liz Patton is one of numerous Camp Bluegrass attendees who have been substantially impacted by their summer experience at South Plains College.

I started on guitar at eleven. This was the thread that started it all, the tiny flake of snow that started the avalanche. My parents played music in high school, but never kept it up. I took some piano lessons when I was about five or six but was bored out of my skull. Nobody in the family played music, just listened to it a lot.

My best friend's dad had recently started playing—first time I'd really seen anyone play anything in person besides piano. Combine that with my love of mid-'90s country—I was smitten. He let me borrow an old clunker of a guitar that I plucked on (with little success) for a little bit, until my grandparents bought me a little 7/8 classical.

[After] *about six months of me trying to work through the* Hal Leonard Guitar Method *on my own, and horribly out-of-tune attempts to play along with whatever musical thing was on the PBS pledge drive at the time, my parents reached back out to my friend's dad, who had started taking lessons from a coworker. Just so happened the teacher was*

Liz Patton at Camp Bluegrass in 2003 with her parents, Rose and Jeff White. *Photo courtesy of Liz Patton.*

Bill Branch. *He played with Mary Hattersley* [a fairly well-known fiddle teacher in the Austin area] *and Lenny Nichols* [a fixture in the Austin bluegrass scene] *in a band called Bill Rowan and the High Rollers. That band never had any particular fame, but the connection with Mary was big. Her Suzuki fiddle students had to perform regularly as part of their learning, so Bill just had his guitar students tag along. Since it's Texas, Mary had a lot of her students playing basic bluegrass songs, Bob Wills tunes and some other more eclectic tunes.*

[At] *one of the student concerts I met Cara Cooke—she played bass and harmonica in and around the Austin bluegrass scene, and she's the one who suggested I check out Camp Bluegrass. This would have been…'98, I think.*[94]

Liz attended Camp Bluegrass for the first time in 2000. She was only fourteen years old, so her mother accompanied her as a chaperone.

The second year, the first afternoon at camp, I walked up to some older gentleman (wish I remembered his name) who was playing bass, and I asked him how does he play that? He said, "It's tuned like the bottom four strings of a guitar" and just handed it to me. I took to it like a duck to water. That sweet man let me steal his bass for the entire week. I was running around with the other youngsters (that's where I met Nate Lee) who would play hookie from class to jam in any corner we could find. That Wednesday night, I remember playing bass while nodding off! I think I gave up about midnight and just slept on the couches in the main dorm center (the name escapes me right now) beside that borrowed bass.[95]

[The] *third year, my parents built my mandobass, and it had just been strung up like the week before camp. Roland White was one of the mandolin teachers that year. He spent all week trying to wheedle me into selling him my bass, because it was small enough that he could play it. I was lucky that year Bill Bryson was back again to teach bass. I still have the workbook he passed out.*

This past summer, I went, and it was so funny the number of times I encountered someone where we'd just look at each other and go, "Don't I know you?" I was amazed how many people recognized me twenty years older, with blue hair, and without the mandobass. She's old and fragile, so Thumper stays home now that I picked up the '56 Kay that's my new workhorse.[96]

Camp Bluegrass in many ways changed the trajectory of my life. It cemented a love of music, it introduced me to people I will never forget, and put me on the path to where I am today. I loved being at South Plains so much I went on to get a bachelor's in jazz at UT–Arlington, where I met my husband, and the brothers who formed the seed of my nonmusical friend group. I may have put the music mostly away for several years— because learning how to be a functional adult with a moderately stable income is tough—but it never stopped. Going back this past summer, I'd forgotten how imbedded the smell of sulfur [from the oil wells] *in the dry panhandle air is in my brain. Bluegrass just hits a different part of my soul when paired with that smell, where I've spent so much time and have so many treasured memories. This year's theme was women in bluegrass, and listening to Anne Luna tell her story was like looking in a funhouse mirror for me. We even were at South Plains together for a year, just in different classes. And being up to my eyeballs in top-tier musicians for a week, I'd forgotten through the years how much that is a core part of who I am, what I love to do. So twenty years after the last time I was at Camp Bluegrass, here it is again, spurring me on into the next phase of my musical "career" because we all know the joke: "How do you make a million dollars playing bluegrass? Start with two million!" I may never have any particular success, but I'll have the time of my life trying!* [97]

Through the decades many outstanding musicians have taught at Camp Bluegrass, include Rolf Sieker, Roger Bush, Herb Pedersen, Raymond McClain, Jim Moratto, Robert Bowlin, Missy Raines, Jon Weisberger, Steve Smith, Tim May and Roland White.

In 2009, Chris Jones brought his whole band, The Night Drivers, to Levelland for Camp Bluegrass. At the time, the band consisted of Ned Luberecki on banjo, Jon Weisberger on bass and Mark Stoffel on mandolin. Besides teaching that week, Jones and Luberecki broadcast their SiriusXM Satellite radio show *Live from Levelland*.

Ned Luberecki discussed Camp Bluegrass on the Banjo Hangout website:

It's one of the most fun music camps that I've ever done. It's [the] great group of people (instructors and students both) that make it such a fun week. And the weather at night is great for outdoor jamming! There's always a beginner class for banjo, and I've actually had students there who were absolute beginners (almost zero knowledge on banjo).

You'll learn maybe a couple of tunes, but more importantly, you'll learn how to jam with others and how to learn. In my classes, I try to guide you into how to learn songs by the melody (by ear) and then how to turn those melodies into banjo solos. You'll also learn about proper technique (how

The Camp Bluegrass advanced guitar glass. *From left to right:* Alex Klein, Liz Patton, Dawson Marrow, Jeff White, Tim May, Mike Kistin, Jerry Scribner and Jim Wagner. *Photo courtesy of Bill Polson.*

to sound better) and maybe most importantly of all, you'll learn from the other students. Learning by doing is the best teacher of all!

I think I can speak for most of the instructors in saying that we are very hands on. Our goal is to get you playing and jamming and having a good time with your instrument. And hopefully inspire you to keep playing. Students usually leave with plenty of handouts and pages of stuff to work on, but it's the hands-on part that (I think) helps the most.[98]

One of the most popular and enjoyable events for the Camp Bluegrass attendees are the Friday morning student concerts. "We usually have about twenty bands that form during the week, so we have to limit them to two songs each!" explained Camp Bluegrass codirector Paula Carr.[99]

Another feature of Camp Bluegrass is a tip of the hat to the past. Every year, the camp pays tribute to the musicians who came before and paved the way. For instance, the 2013 camp was a tribute to Earl Scruggs, and the 2016 camp featured the music of Jim & Jesse and the Virginia Boys, while the 2018 camp featured the music of the Kentucky Colonels, a fitting tribute to Roland and Clarence White.

A new tradition at Camp Bluegrass is the annual highly anticipated performance of Kitty Starr and the Whereabouts. Kitty Starr is the alias of banjo instructor Beth Mead. Her longtime partners in rhyme include Anne Luna on bass, Chris Sanders on guitar, Dede Wyland on guitar and other female musicians at Camp Bluegrass, including Becky Buller. "They come together as women from different bands during Camp Bluegrass to bring some female-led songs and comedy to the evening, usually dressing in silly costumes and using props," said Jade Throneberry.[100]

When COVID-19 brought the world to a halt in the spring of 2020, Alan Munde and Paula Carr discussed their options. There were thoughts of going online, similar to the route taken by the Augusta Heritage Center in West Virginia.[101] "Alan and I discussed an online option, but everyone wanted to be together."[102]

The school postponed Camp Bluegrass for 2020 and 2021 for COVID concerns, Munde explained. "We will resume this year. Paula Carr and I have continued with the support of the administration of South Plains College. Without the school's support, we could not have survived the pandemic."[103]

Paula said the 2022 camp was a great success. Camp Bluegrass hosted 125 students from across the country and around the world. "There were a few challenges. The thought of COVID-19 was on our minds, and that caused a bit of stress. Some teachers talked about their concern about COVID

A late-night jam at Camp Bluegrass. *Photo courtesy of Liz Patton.*

outbreaks at other camps. Luckily, we only had one. We also had a few instructors insist on wearing masks, and we respected that; after all, this is how they make their living, and they want to stay healthy. The students were cooperative also when the instructors required masks."[104]

In 2022, the instructors included Nate Lee, Becky Buller, Dan Boner, Ned Luberecki, Missy Raines, Gerald Jones, Bill Evans, Beath Mead, Dede Wyland, Dave Polston and Elliott Rogers. Like Jade Thornberry, Elliott is another Camp Bluegrass student who became an instructor.

For more information on Camp Bluegrass, see:
campbluegrass.com
South Plains College Continuing Education
1401 College Ave.
Levelland, Texas 79336
(806) 894-9611 ext. 2341

HIGH PLAINS JAMBOREE

It was a hot summer evening in Gruene, Texas. Music from the historic Gruene Hall sliced through the heavy Texas air in old downtown Gruene. Stepping inside Gruene Hall did not bring any relief from the heat. Visitors fanned themselves as water droplets rolled down cold bottles of beer. Three musicians were gathered around one giant, vintage microphone, their western shirts soaked with perspiration. The three of them must have played over forty songs that night to a small but enthusiastic audience.

They called themselves High Plains Jamboree. What would you call their music? "It's been said that High Plains Jamboree is a bluegrass band west of the Mississippi and a country band east of the Mississippi."[105] That's the statement on their old BandsInTown page. Why don't we call it prairie grass?

The members of High Plains Jamboree were Brennen Leigh on mandolin and vocals, Simon Flory on bass and guitar and Noel McKay on bass and guitar. The Austin-based group started in 2015.

North Dakota born and Minnesota raised, Brennen Leigh began performing at the age of fourteen. When she turned nineteen she took her country song bag to Austin, Texas. Before High Plains Jamboree came together, Brennen recorded solo six albums, one with Jesse Dayton and two with Noel McKay.

Simon Flory was born in rural Indiana. He moved to Chicago after college, starting the country band Merle the Mule and teaching at the Old Town School of Folk Music. Then, in 2008, he moved south to Arkansas,

Left: High Plains Jamboree
performing at Gruene Hall.
Photo courtesy of Jeff Campbell.

Below: Three talented musicians
(*from left to right*): Brennen Leigh,
Simon Flory and Noel McKay.
Photo courtesy of Jeff Campbell.

working with and learning from his friend and mentor the late Donny Catron. Danny was a member of the famed bluegrass band the Tennessee Gentlemen. *Unholy Town*, his first solo album, led him to Austin.

Noel McKay, the only native Texan in the band, was raised in Lubbock and the Texas Hill Country. Noel was "discovered" by the legendary Texas songwriter Guy Clark at a performance in Kerrville. He and his brother, Hollin, formed the McKay Brothers band. The brothers released two albums in the 2000s, the self-titled *McKay Brothers* and *Cold Beer & Hot Tamales*. The brothers had numerous red dirt regional hit songs during this time.

The band also featured fiddlers Beth Chrisman and Andy Lentz.

For two and a half years, High Plains Jamboree were coming in hot. They played all across the country and toured the United Kingdom, mining a similar musical vein as the Carolina Chocolate Drops, the Devil Makes Three and Old Crow Medicine Show.

High Plains Jamboree played the 2016 AmericanaFest, where *Rolling Stone* magazine called the band part of the "20 Best Things We Saw": "Like many of their Americana peers, country-grass quartet High Plains Jamboree celebrate days of old. In the song 'Analog,' a smart but sweet tune calling out 'advertisements on my telephone' and GMOs, mandolin player Brennen Leigh croons, 'I'm not down on it just because it's new.' But few do it with as much verve as this Austin, Texas, foursome."[106]

In 2017 the band headed east and performed at the IBMA World of Bluegrass. The band released one album, the self-titled CD *High Plains Jamboree*. Songs on the album included "It Never Rains," "Georgia Mules and Country Boys," "Dollar Bill," "Putting Up a Front," "When Country Isn't Cool Anymore," "Smartphone" and "Change the Oil."

On February 11, 2018, High Plains Jamboree announced on their Twitter feed that they were calling it quits as a band. As Simon Flory stated, "There was a little cascade of a downfall kind of thing."[107]

Simon Flory settled in Fort Worth, Texas. "Austin is too monochromatic for me," Flory says. "Everybody's sort of the same. People would say, 'Well, you can't really go anywhere else in Texas, right? This is the only cool town.' I've always replied, 'No, there's a town that's cooler than this. It's called Fort Worth.' You got some weird dichotomies here, man. This place is way weirder than Austin."[108]

Brennen and Noel, who were partners long before High Plains Jamboree, headed to Nashville.

Simon went on to release two albums, *Radioville* and *Haul These Blues Away*. He would also release two EPs, *Young Giants* (featuring Fort Worth accordion sensation Ginny Mac) and *Paper Thin Lines*. *Paper Thin Lines* was released with a short documentary film.

Brennen Leigh recorded two critically acclaimed albums: *Prairie Love Letter*, an homage to her beloved homeland, and *Obsessed with the West*, one of the best western swing albums since Bob Wills hung up his fiddle. *Obsessed with the West* featured Brennen's western swing mentor Ray Benson and his band Asleep at the Wheel.

Noel McKay also released a critically acclaimed album, *Blue Blue Blue*. Noel continues to write songs and perform as a duo with Brennen.

Simon, Brennen and Noel have obviously gone on to have successful music careers. Some of us can say, "I remember when they played in that band High Plains Jamboree."

FROM GRAPELAND TO AUSTIN:
AN INTERVIEW WITH ANDI JO IIUFF

Andi Jo Huff was born in East Texas close to Salmon Lake Park in Grapeland. Salmon Lake Park is legendary for their bluegrass festivals held throughout the year. Born into a musical family, it was here at Salmon Lake where Andi became an accomplished musician.

Her music career started with her family's bluegrass band, Hwy 19, and she presently plays fiddle and sings with Austin's Hillsiders. The Hillsiders, like Audie Blaylock and Redline, have their own coffee brand. What is it about bluegrass bands and coffee?

The following interview was conducted by Jeff Campbell in the summer of 2022.

The family bluegrass band, Hwy 19. How many family members were in the band and what instruments did they play?

The original band roster consisted of four family members of mine, my mother, stepdad and Aunt Frances. My mother, Tammy Hassell-Anderson, plays guitar and sings lead vocals; my stepdad, Dr. Stuart Anderson, plays banjo; and my aunt Frances (who is everyone's Aunt Frances) played bass and sang harmony during her time in the group. The current Hwy 19 roster is my mom, Stuart and Jeff Harrison (of Buffalo, Texas) on the upright bass.

Left: Andi Jo Huff. *Photo courtesy of Andi Jo Huff.*

Right: Andi Jo, jamming with the family. *Photo courtesy of Andi Jo Huff.*

Who were some of your fiddle teachers?

I started playing fiddle at eight years old and took my first lessons from Ms. Patsy Saucier, a violinist in Grapeland, Texas. She worked with me for over a year and soon realized that I was no violinist. She told my mother that playing fiddle was my only option because of how fast I learned by ear. I'm sure my mom was pleased to hear this because she was also learning rhythm guitar at the time.

After this, we struggled to find fiddle teachers in the local area, so my mom started to drive me to Lufkin every week to meet with JC Haunschel. JC was a family friend of ours from Salmon Lake Park, and he taught for about another year, maybe a little more.

My third fiddle teacher and my last was Kevin Carter of Lufkin. He was more of a swing, classic country fiddle player, which was new to me. This arrangement didn't last very long, and that's the end of my fiddle lessons. Most of my fiddle playing is self-taught and heavily relies on my ear and basic music theory.

Your website talks about church, hymnal singing and family harmonies. How young were you when you started?

I started singing as early as I can remember. I was the kid who loved to perform and wasn't a bit shy. My mom and Aunt Frances were good to create opportunities for me to sing in front of family, [at] church and [at] nursing homes.

Who were some of your mentors, and how did they influence your musicianship?

I'm thankful to have several mentors both musically and personally. My mom bought me my first "made in China" fiddle shortly after I blurted, "I want to play the fiddle!" out of the blue. She drove me to fiddle lessons for four years, learned guitar to back me up and encouraged me to practice consistently because "no one regrets learning an instrument when they're old." I wouldn't be where I am today if it weren't for my mom's support and encouragement.

Aunt Frances is another musical mentor of mine. To this day, I haven't met anyone with a better ear for harmony than Frances Jordan. Not only can she hear every note in a chord that should be played and sung, but she can organize those thoughts and teach others to sing it. Singing with Aunt Frances in Hwy 19 and church was a major influence in how I sing with others today. She would say, "Close harmony is preferred," "Listen to each other and make your voices ONE" and, of course, "That's not in the chord." I learned a lot from Aunt Frances.

Another person who is of great influence in my life is Stuart Anderson. Stuart is my stepdad, bluegrass mentor, professional mentor and dear friend. He is a recently retired mathematics professor, and I actually took two courses from him in college. Yes, he is a banjo-playing mathematician, which throws all the banjo jokes out the window. Stuart has influenced me in so many ways. He has always been eager to analyze a song or musical concept with me. He's the one I go to right after I learn or write a new song. We share music, ideas, challenges and his opinion is trusted. I wish everyone could have a Stuart Anderson in their life.

The Southern Gospel School of Music. What was that experience like and how did it affect your musicianship?

Texas Southern Gospel School of Music and singing in church is where it all started. My first year at music school was age seven, and I attended until

I was thirteen or fourteen. Music school is where I learned the basic music theory and how to sing harmony. Before this summer camp, I could only match a note when singing, not sing the third or fifth of the chord. I sang alto in the music school choir and sat next to Linda Louis, who wrote music for convention singing hymnals and was very good at sight reading. She would help me find the right notes, and I'm convinced that music school is where I learned how to find harmony. In addition to music school, I would often sing with my mother and the Daniels Sisters, which was made up of Frances Jordan, Louis Hassell (my grandmother) and Rita Moore (my aunt). They are well-known in the Houston County area for their family harmony and singing in church throughout the area. Some of my fondest memories are singing southern gospel music with my family.

The Salmon Lake Park festivals: Was this a family tradition, and who were some of the folks you learned from?

Salmon Lake Park is adjacent to my homeplace in Grapeland, Texas, and we would go to the gospel and bluegrass festivals each year. This is where I learned how to play fiddle in a bluegrass jam. I grew up playing with Lynn Grey, Donna Mobley and her son Jed, Larry Burnside, Jeff Harrison and Dennis Conn, to name a few.

What led you to move to Austin?

I graduated from SMU with a math degree in 2015 and found a job working for a financial technology company in Austin starting in February 2016. I moved here right after college.

In Austin who have you played with and who have you learned from?

Since finding my bluegrass community in Austin, I've made huge progress in my musical journey by surrounding myself with such talented musicians. My first bluegrass pal was David McDonald of Steel Betty, and he introduced me to everyone else. I was introduced to and played with BJ Lazarus, Devon Canady, Hunter Hollingsworth, Matt Downing and Phillip Brush in the very beginning. I've met many other phenomenal musicians after playing more gigs and networking within the community.

Above: The Hillsiders. *From left to right*: Hunter Hollingsworth, Dom Fisher, Andi Jo and Devon Canady. *Photo courtesy of Andi Jo Huff.*

Left: Coffee and bluegrass, from the Hillsiders. *Photo courtesy of Andi Jo Huff.*

How did the Hillsiders come about?

The Hillsiders came about during the pandemic. The 2020 Salmon Lake Bluegrass Festival and 2020 Mill Fest in Kennard, Texas, both experienced several band cancellations for obvious reasons. Both events were in need of a band, so I put one together. The Hillsiders was originally called the Bluegrass Pals and started as a six piece in the Salmon Lake Park festival. As the vision became clear and our goals aligned, we eventually renamed the group to the Hillsiders, and it became a four-piece band consisting of Dom Fisher, Devon Canady, Hunter Hollingsworth and myself.

LIKE MOST BUSINESSES, THE COVID-19 era wreaked havoc on the music industry. Concerts were canceled, staff were out of work and venues sat empty. The Hillsiders are an example of something good coming out of a period of darkness. Their fresh take that combines old-time and bluegrass styles is a breath of fresh air. The Hillsiders are releasing their first album in 2023.

THE LONE STAR GUITAR PRODIGY

Guitarist Derek Trucks played his first paid gig at eleven years old and, by the time he was thirteen, was opening for the Allman Brothers. Jazz guitarist Julian Lage played on the Grammy Awards show at the age of twelve, and three years later, he found himself at Stanford University, not as a student, but as a faculty member of the Stanford Jazz Workshop. At the age of nineteen, Billy Strings started playing professionally with mandolist Don Julin (the author of *Mandolin for Dummies*). In 2022, a Texan from Georgetown, Texas, threw his hat into the guitar prodigy ring.

On April 9, 2022, the Bluegrass Heritage Foundation held its annual Texas State Championships for banjo, mandolin and guitar. A nervous young guitarist waited patiently for his turn in the spotlight. He had only been flat picking for about a year and knew the other competitors were more experienced. As he waited, he prayed and then stepped on the stage. When the competition was completed, the judges chose thirteen-year-old Parker Jensen as the 2022 Texas State Champion!

It takes a lot of dedication and practice to become a Texas State Guitar Champion, but it also helps to have family support and mentorship. Parker's sister plays a variety of instruments, such as mandolin, guitar, bass and keyboard, and his dad plays the bass.

Parker has also been fortunate to study under some pretty talented folks:

> *I have taken lessons from John Young, Jimmy T, Aaron Kemkaran, Brian and Andrew Wilson. John is family to us so he helped to get into a*

Charlotte and Parker Jensen. *Photo courtesy of Parker Jensen.*

bluegrass / bluegrass gospel band called Jam Pak ran by Mrs. Anni Beach. Jimmy T helped me with getting my rhythm better and up to par with other players. Aaron Kemkaran helped me with lead work and is currently working with me on recording with logic pro. Brian put me in a little band where we just learned songs that we liked, and he helped me with my guitar lead as well. We met Andrew where he ran Wilsons School of Strings, and I learned to play bluegrass, jazz, country lead and fiddle. And he helped me with a lot of hurdles along the way with business and relationships with other musicians.[109]

The music community in Georgetown has also been supportive of Parker's music. The people who have given him advice on gear, strings and the music business include Anji Pearl and Charlie Day, Izaak Mora, Matt Downing, Andrew Wilson, Angelyn Iturbide, Cam Dozier, Kyle Piland, Sam Grona, Chris and Emily Hamilton and Elle Townley. Parker is also paying it forward by teaching music to people at his local church.

Parker Jensen has a bright future, and by the time you hold this book in your hands, he'll probably have added a few more chapters to his story!

PICKIN' ON THE SQUARE

Jim Paul's [Miller] passion for bluegrass music ran deep and strong. I played in many a jam session with him, and he'd grin the whole time through a song, but when it came time for him to sing, his booming voice could bring the rafters down. He held nothing back, and that's how he made such a difference within the bluegrass scene. He cared about getting everyone involved, making sure that everyone could participate in whatever way they could. All in the name of bluegrass.
—Missy Raines[110]

The musical history of Garland, Texas, dates all the way back to 1906, when the Garland Coronet Band was formed to give public performances around town. In the many decades to follow, more groups were founded and eventually concert venues were opened, creating more opportunities for citizens to enjoy live musical presentations. One such venue was the Garland Opry, a small venue that opened its downtown doors in 1974. While it gave future country stars such as LeAnn Rimes their first taste of performing in front of an audience, it also played a small role in the beginning of one of the longest-running bluegrass gatherings in North Texas.

Jim Paul Miller was born on October 22, 1934, in Athens, Texas. In 1944, he and his family moved to the town of Garland, where he would remain the rest of his life. Although he owned and operated the Miller Electric Company for his occupation, music was one of his first loves, something he had been exposed to from an early age. As his daughter DeJean remembered: "In the

Jim Paul Miller brought many pickers and singers together on the square in downtown Garland on Saturday nights. *Photo courtesy of Paula Miller Newman.*

'30s and '40s, a couple of his uncles formed a group, and a couple of his grandfathers did music of one kind or another; I think one played the guitar. When I was a little girl in the '60s, Dad would sing and try to play the one song he knew, 'I Dream of Jeanie with the Light Brown Hair.'"[111]

It wasn't until Jim Paul became acquainted with his daughter-in-law Kathy's family that he discovered his love for bluegrass music. "He was in his sixties," his wife, Shirley, recalled. "Our son's wife's mother and her brothers all played bluegrass music, and he would go over and visit with Kathy's mother and daddy. He saw her guitar and mandolin sitting around, and they started talking music. She started teaching him different things and of course lots of bluegrass songs, so they got a little group together and played in living rooms for two or three years."[112]

Pretty soon, Jim Paul began attending the monthly jam sessions at the Southwest Bluegrass Club. It was these meetings that inspired him to bring bluegrass music to Garland. "The director of Garland Parks and Recreation was in one of the country music bands and we were friends with him. So he kind of got in with the country music (Garland Opry) group, helped them wire a building and get it ready. They made an auditorium out of this store in Downtown Garland. They played there a few times, and it sort of wasn't working out real good because the country group wanted to play the same times that the bluegrass musicians wanted to play. So he decided to move outside," Shirley recollected.[113]

Pretty soon, the Saturday night jam sessions at the Garland Square had grown in popularity. "Word got around and people were calling wanting to know when we were playing. It kept the phone pretty busy in those early years. Until he [Jim Paul] passed away, we would have four and five different groups of musicians playing and lots of people around listening. The die-hard bluegrassers in the early years would sometimes play 'til four or five o'clock in the morning."[114]

The Garland Square soon became a hub for bluegrass musicians young and old, no matter where they were in their playing ability, to come together and learn from each other. One of those pickers was Gary Penny, who began attending the Garland Square jams in the early 1990s: "I had taken the family downtown to the Garland Opry. We went in at about 5:00, came out at about 7:00; man there was like 250 people out at the square. I was like, 'What in the heck?' There were guitars, mandolins and basses. He [Jim Paul] saw me, and he goes, 'Hey, man, what are you doing?' I was like, 'I don't know, man, what you are doing?' He said, 'We do this every Saturday night. Do you play?' I said, 'Well, I play a little guitar.' Now when I say play guitar, I didn't even own or know what a capo was." With Jim Paul's encouragement and friendship, Gary soon developed his abilities as a bluegrass guitarist and mandolinist.[115]

Another way in which Jim Paul helped his fellow musicians learn their craft was by bringing in professional bluegrass artists to perform concerts and give educational workshops in downtown Garland. One such artist was Grammy-nominated bassist Missy Raines: "We would drive all the way from Nashville to be part of one of his shows because we knew that he would take care of us and that he would have worked hard to make sure everything was good. He spent days ahead of time making the best Texas brisket I have ever eaten *to this day*, while his lovely wife, Shirley, made sure every other side dish you could imagine was perfectly made and ready to go. That's just what they did. They didn't just present concerts, start jam sessions and organize workshops; they created a community, they fostered that community and nurtured it."[116] Other notable artists that Miller brought to Garland include the Chicks (formerly known as the Dixie Chicks), Special Consensus and Russell Moore and IIIrd Tyme Out.

On September 13, 2007, at the age of seventy-two, Jim Paul Miller passed away after a short bout with cancer and other health issues.

Even after his passing, the high lonesome sound of the music Miller loved continues to fill the downtown Garland Square every Saturday night from April through October. His legacy has also continued with the Jim Paul Miller Memorial Scholarship, which has provided youth musicians with the opportunity to hone their craft at music camps around Texas. It's a testament to his role as a "bluegrass evangelist," which Gary Penny refers to him as. "He truly wanted you to get involved and appreciated whatever you did. He didn't want to judge people on their playing. He really just wanted to judge them on their enthusiasm."[117]

JADE THRONEBERRY'S FULL PLATE

J ade Throneberry was born in Abilene, Texas, in 2002. A year later, her family relocated to Artesia, New Mexico. It was there that Jade started taking piano lessons at the age of three. However, it was a trip to Lubbock, three years later, that changed her musical path.

Jade and her family attended a concert in Lubbock, Texas, at the historic Cactus Theater. No one in the family can remember the name of the band that day. What is remembered about the concert is that was the day that Jade became enthralled with the sound of fiddle. Jade made her mind up, at the young age of six, that she was going to be a fiddle player.

When the holidays rolled around, Jade found a fiddle under the Christmas tree. She soon started taking lessons with Laine Rountree. At the age of twelve, Jade started learning the mandolin.

Jade also became a regular at Camp Bluegrass in Levelland, Texas. She spent her first six years as a student and then one year (2019) as an assistant fiddle instructor. In 2022, she taught beginning guitar, an instrument she learned to play during the pandemic. Jade felt the guitar would be better suited for her solo performances. She also enrolled in the commercial music program at South Plains College in Levelland.

Her family had relocated to Wolfforth, Texas (just outside of Lubbock), and Jade became a utility player for bands and musicians in the Lubbock area. She has played with Spur 327, Flatland Bluegrass and Jordan Robert Kirk. Like Camp Bluegrass and college, these have also been learning opportunities for Jade.

Flatland Bluegrass is a bluegrass band that was started by brothers Jeff and Randy Redman in 1977, and they're still going strong. Different members have come and gone over the years, but the constants are Jeff (mandolin/harmony vocals) and Randy (banjo/vocals). The other current members are David Barnett (guitar/vocals) and, of course, Jade on fiddle and vocals.

"I've learned a zillion songs playing with Flatland Bluegrass!" exclaimed Jade. "Since I have been with the band we have practiced every week for the

FLATLAND BLUEGRASS

Opposite, top: Jade Throneberry playing the fiddle. *Photo courtesy of Jade Throneberry.*

Opposite, bottom: Jade Throneberry. *Photo courtesy of Jade Throneberry.*

Left: The debut album by Flatland Bluegrass, 1979. *Author's collection.*

Below: Flatland Bluegrass performing at the Plains Watermelon Festival in 2022. *Courtesy Flatland Bluegrass.*

past three years. Before I joined the band, they had practiced every week for fifteen years! I also have gotten my guitar-style learning from Randy. David has also taught me singing harmony and how to 'mike' a bluegrass band, which can be challenging."

Playing in Jordan Robert Kirk's band has also been a learning experience. Jordan Robert is a Texas singer/songwriter, who like Lyle Lovett and Robert Earl Keen can't be slotted into a particular genre. Jade specifically mentioned Jordan Robert's bass player and producer, Sean Fankhauser.

"John taught me about being a part of a team on stage. Working as a unit and moving the band forward."

At Camp Bluegrass, Jade was able to play with the Hard Road Trio and some special guests. The Hard Road Trio, based in Las Cruces, New Mexico, consists of Anne Luna on bass and vocals; Steve Smith on mandolin, vocals and octave mando; and Chris Sanders on guitar and vocals. Their desert grass sound is a blend of bluegrass, folk music and jazz. The special guests included Texan Nate Lee on fiddle and Ned Luberecki on banjo. With Jade on vocals the collective did an outstanding version of the Kansas song "Carry On My Wayward Son." Jade and the "Super Group" created a fresh take on a classic rock classic. "That was the most talented band I have ever played with!" said Jade.[118]

In 2019 and 2020, she was an assistant to Nate Lee, instructing at the Desert Night Acoustic Music Camp in Tucson, Arizona.

For such a young musician, Jade has had the opportunity to play with a wide range of talented folks. She looks forward to playing with many other musicians whom she admires. "My dream collaboration would be with Alan Jackson. I have been a big Alan Jackson fan since I was little. I've seen him

Jade Throneberry and friends, backstage. *Photo courtesy of Jade Throneberry.*

Ned Luberecki and
Jade Throneberry.
*Photo courtesy of Jade
Throneberry.*

in concert seven times. That opportunity may not ever come about because it looks like he's about to retire," said Jade.[119]

Jade also mentions Hayward County, North Carolina's Balsam Range and the Billy Strings Band as wo bands she would love to collaborate with. Jade had the opportunity to interview Balsam Range fiddler and vocalist Buddy Melton and Billy Strings bassist Royal Masat as part of a college course.

Jade is currently enrolled in the joint commercial music program at South Plains College and Texas Tech University. Her intention after graduation is to enroll in the Appalachian Studies–Bluegrass Master's program at East Tennessee State University in Johnson City, Tennessee. Alumni of ETSU include Amythyst Kiah, Barry Bales, Becky Buller, Matt Wright, Tim Stafford, Tray Wellington and Wesley Carr.

If that's not enough of a full plate, Jade also assists her father with construction projects. She has taken on everything from sheetrock, tiling, flooring and painting to electrical installations. "We have remodeled every house we have lived in and built the house we live in now," said Jade.[120] On top of that, Jade teaches fiddle online and in person through her company Western Strings Music.

As you read this, take a moment to Google "Jade Throneberry." There is no telling what she has on her plate today!

PLAY IT FORWARD

There is nothing more sad or glorious than generations changing hands.
—John Mellencamp[121]

As the Texas heat subsides and the cool autumn winds blow, bluegrass fans and musicians make an annual pilgrimage to Farmers Branch, Texas. The Bloomin' Bluegrass Festival is held every October at the city's Historical Park.

The festival, organized by the Bluegrass Heritage Foundation, brings the very best of the bluegrass world to North Texas. Walking away from the main stage, you're still surrounded by music. Jam sessions are going on all through the park. Young and old, friends and family, novice and expert are playing the music they love. Not for fame or money, but just the sheer joy of making music together.

Bloomin' Bluegrass is one of the many endeavors of the Bluegrass Heritage Foundation. Led by Alan Tompkins, the nonprofit produces many events throughout the year. The biggest of these are the Bluegrass Heritage Festival, the Wylie Jubilee Bluegrass on Ballard and Bluegrass Saturday Night in McKinney.

Another pillar of the Bluegrass Heritage Foundation is the Play It Forward program. Play It Forward is a musical instrument lending program that "helps foster music literacy and performance skills in deserving young people (ages 8–21) by providing no-cost access to the primary bluegrass musical instruments such as mandolins, fiddles, banjos, guitars, and resonator guitars."[122]

Braeden Paul and Lloyd Bilyeu. Though he makes his home in Garland, Texas, Lloyd hails from Kentucky, where he performed on the radio as a youngster. *Photo courtesy of Robby Paul.*

The Play It Forward program, along with Camp Bluegrass in Levelland and the Central Texas Bluegrass Association's Willa Beach-Porter Scholarship Program, is a big reason for the growth of bluegrass in the state of Texas.

The state of Texas abounds with young bluegrass musicians, such as Jade Throneberry, Parker Jensen and Riley Gilbreath. At the same time, we mourn the loss of folks like Byron Berline (fiddle virtuoso who played with everyone from Bill Monroe to the Rolling Stones), Bob Gates (the super volunteer with the Bluegrass Heritage Foundation), Tootie Williams (bass player for the Stone Mountain Boys), Harry S. Hendry Jr. (multi-instrumentalist with the Bluegrass Wranglers) and the many others who have gone before us.

However, this traditional music form lives on every time a kid picks up an instrument.

Play It Forward.

NOTES

Preface

1. "Billy Strings—Long Journey Home (Official Video)—ME/AND/ DAD," YouTube, accessed November 22, 2022, https://www.youtube. com/watch?v=S9E8CWXjkAw&t=14s.
2. In the coastal fishing industry *fisherman* is a gender-neutral term referring to men and women.

Riley Gilbreath

3. Riley Gilbreath, phone interview with author, November 1, 2022.
4. Jim Penson, email interview with author, November 2, 2022.
5. Ibid.
6. Riley, interview.
7. John Lawless, "Bluegrass Heritage Foundation Gets Riley Gilbreath a New Huber Banjo," *Bluegrass Today*, December 28, 2017, https:// bluegrasstoday.com/bluegrass-heritage-foundation-gets-riley-gilbreath-a-new-huber-banjo/.
8. Riley, interview.
9. Ibid.
10. Ibid.
11. Penson, interview.

Banjo Ben and the Purple Hulls

12. Alia Pappas, "Two Peas in a Pod: The Purple Hulls Serve Up Southern Acoustic Roots Music," *County Line Magazine*, April 24, 2017.

13. Nigel Cliff, *Moscow Nights: The Van Cliburn Story—How One Man and His Piano Transformed the Cold War* (New York: HarperCollins, 2016); Stuart Isacoff, *When the World Stopped to Listen: Van Cliburn's Cold War Triumph, and Its Aftermath* (New York: Knopf, 2017).

14. Ken Beck, "Banjo Ben Clark Shares His Music Around the World," Wilson Post, updated March 31, 2022, https://www.wilsonpost.com/news/banjo-ben-clark-shares-his-music-around-the-world/article_fc3bc328-7529-11eb-a9ef-2b48839cb668.html.

15. Katy Lou Clark, email interview with author, September 26, 2022.

16. Ibid.

17. Penny Clark, email interview with author, October 10, 2022.

18. Ben Clark, interview by Matthew Davis, Banjo Newsletter, August 2020, https://banjonews.com/2020-08/banjo_ben_clark_interview_by_matthew_davis.html.

19. Ben Clark, interview by the author, October 10, 2022.

20. Ibid.

21. Ibid.

22. Janelle Landauer, "BANJO BEN CLARK: Taylor Swift Makes 'Life on the Road as Easy as Possible' for the Band," Countrymusiconline.net, May 10, 2008, http://www.countrymusiconline.net/banjobenclark.html.

23. Ben Clark, interview.

24. Katy Lou Clark, interview.

25. Penny Clark, interview.

26. Ben Clark, interview.

27. Katy Lou Clark, interview.

28. Ibid.

29. Penny Clark, interview.

30. Ibid.

31. Katy Lou Clark, interview.

The Cooke Brothers

32. *Corsicana Semi-Weekly Light*, July 5, 1949.

33. Carolyn Wills, "The Real Deals," *Waxahachie NOW*, August 3, 2015.

34. Snuffy Jenkins Festival Facebook page, 2014, accessed November 5, 2022, https://www.facebook.com/profile.php?id=100063138255145.
35. Wills, "Real Deals."
36. Sandra McIntosh, "No Longer Tied Down," *Waxahachie NOW*, November 2008.
37. Ibid.
38. Billy Joe Cooke, email interview with the author, September 19, 2022.

Born in Texas

39. *Cambridge Essential English Dictionary*, 2nd ed. (Cambridge: Cambridge University Press, 2011).
40. Billy Bright is another bluegrass artist from El Paso. A mandolinist, Billy attended the Berklee College of Music and has played with Tony Rice, Peter Rowan, Norman Blake and the Grammy-nominated bluegrass band Wood & Wire. Billy has also released two critically acclaimed albums with banjo virtuoso Alan Munde.
41. Jacques Dicroce, "A Conversation with Audie Blaylock," Hudson Valley Bluegrass Association, February 24, 2012.
42. Ibid.
43. Audie Blaylock, interview with the author, July 18, 2022.
44. Dicroce, "Conversation with Audie Blaylock."
45. Blaylock, interview.

Jesse Brock (C.W. Brock Family)

46. Jesse Brock, email interview with author, July 6, 2022.
47. Ibid.
48. Daniel Patrick (host), "Episode #59: Jesse Brock," *Mandolins and Beer Podcast*, September 15, 2020, https://podcasts.apple.com/us/podcast/the-mandolins-and-beer-podcast-episode-59-jesse-brock/id1474010499?i=1000491398548.
49. Brock, interview.
50. Ibid.

The Davis Brothers (Greg and Brad)

51. Greg Davis, phone interview with author, July 20, 2022.
52. Alison Richter, "Brad Davis: 'The Rhythmic Underbelly, That Fabric, Is the Key to Better Lead Playing,'" musicradar, July 3, 2018, https://www.musicradar.com/news/brad-davis-the-rhythmic-underbelly-that-fabric-is-the-key-to-better-lead-playing.
53. Davis, interview.
54. Ibid.
55. Brad Davis official website, www.braddavismusic.com.

Chuck Lee: Santa Makes Banjos

56. "Ovilla, Texas Population 2022," World Population Review, accessed November 28, 2022, https://worldpopulationreview.com/us-cities/ovilla-tx-population.
57. Chuck Lee Banjo Company website, www.chuckleebanjos.blogspot.com.
58. You can learn more about Nate Lee in *Texas Bluegrass History: High Lonesome on the High Plains* (The History Press, 2021).
59. Chuck Lee official website, "About Santa Chuck Lee," accessed November 28, 2022, https://chuckleeinc.com/about-santa-chuck-lee.

The Pyeatt Family

60. "Obituary," Lugienbuel Funeral Home, accessed November 15, 2022, http://www.luginbuel.com/deceased-records/person/tilman-franklin-pyeatt-1933-2007. Tilman Pyeatt died on January 24, 2007.
61. "Obituary," J.E. Foust & Son Funeral Directors, accessed November 15, 2022, https://www.dignitymemorial.com/obituaries/grapevine-tx/lena-cramer-9960496. Lena Cramer died on December 21, 2020.
62. R. Moag, "The History of Early Bluegrass in Texas," *Journal of Texas Music History* 4, no. 2 (2004): 22–48.
63. "Obituary," J.E. Foust & Son Funeral Directors, accessed November 15, 2022, https://www.dignitymemorial.com/obituaries/grapevine-tx/marilyn-fry-8132646. Marilyn Fry died on January 18, 2019.

The Steel Drivin' Fiddler

64. Tammy Rogers, email interview with author, October 12, 2022.

65. Ibid.

66. Ibid.

67. Ibid.

68. Ibid.

69. Tammy Rogers official website, www.tammyrogers.com.

70. Tammy Rogers, "DittyTV's INSIGHTS: Tammy Rogers," interview conducted by Amy Wright, DittyTV, 2022, https://podcasts.apple.com/us/podcast/tammy-rogers/id1516722465?i=1000500818632.

71. John Lawless, "A New Chapter for The Steeldrivers," *Bluegrass Today*, December 21, 2011, https://bluegrasstoday.com/a-new-chapter-for-the-steeldrivers/.

The Vestal Brothers (Scott and Curtis)

72. Curtis Vestal, phone interview with author, June 8, 2022.

73. Scott Vestal, email interview with author, February 28, 2021.

74. Curtis Vestal, interview.

75. Scott Vestal official website, www.scottvestal.com.

76. Scott Vestal, interview.

77. Curtis Vestal, interview.

The Whites

78. Jay Cridlin, "Ry Cooder Out to Revive Country Music with Ricky Skaggs, Sharon White," *Tampa Bay Times*, March 30, 2016, https://www.tampabay.com/things-to-do/music/ry-cooder-out-to-revive-country-music-with-ricky-skaggs-sharon-white/2271253/.

79. Bluegrass Music Hall of Fame and Museum Oral History Project, interview with Buck White, February 19, 2010, Louie B. Nunn Center for Oral History, University of Kentucky Libraries Bill Davis, Interviewer | 2018oh281_ibmm075.

80. Ibid.

81. Rod Moag, with Alta Campbell, "The History of Early Bluegrass in Texas," *Journal of Texas Music History* 4, no. 2: 23–48, https://gato-docs.

its.txstate.edu/center-for-texas-music-history/journals/volume-4-no2/
Volume_4_No_2_The-History-of-Early-Bluegrass-in-Texas/Volume_4_
No_2_.
82. Bluegrass Music Hall of Fame and Museum Oral History Project,
interview with Buck White.
83. Kevin John Coyne, "100 Greatest Women, #80: Sharon and Cheryl
White (The Whites)," CountryUniverse, April 22, 2018, http://www.
countryuniverse.net/2018/04/22/100-greatest-women-80-sharon-and-
cheryl-white-the-whites/.
84. Chuck Dauphin, "Ricky Skaggs & Sharon White Talk New Album 'Hearts
Like Ours,'" *Billboard*, October 1, 2014, https://www.billboard.com/music/
country/ricky-skaggs-sharon-white-hearts-like-ours-interview-6266825/.

A Dawg and a Herd of Longhorns

85. Matthew Lyons, "Bluegrass Beginnings and the Start of Burnt Orange
Bluegrass," spring 2018, emailed to author, May 12, 2022.
86. Amy Rester, email interview with the author, May 28, 2022.
87. Ibid.
88. Ibid.

Camp Bluegrass at South Plains College

89. Jade Throneberry, Instagram interview with the author, August 16,
2022.
90. You can read more about the South Plains College bluegrass and music
programs in *Texas Bluegrass History*.
91. Campbell and Paul, *Texas Bluegrass History*, 58.
92. Paula Carr, interview with the author, September 15, 2022.
93. Alex Driggars, "Musicians from Around Region and Globe Visit
Levelland for Camp Bluegrass," *Lubbock Avalanche-Journal*, July 25 2022.
94. Liz Patton, email interview with the author, August 29, 2022.
95. Ibid.
96. Ibid.
97. Ibid.
98. Banjo Hangout, Discussion Forum, accessed August 5, 2022, https://
www.banjohangout.org/archive/276044.

99. Carr, interview.

100. Throneberry, Instagram interview.

101. Alex Hines, "D&E's August Summer Sessions Moves Online for 2020," 12WBOY, July 2, 2020, https://www.wboy.com/news/randolph/des-augusta-summer-sessions-moves-online-for-2020.

102. Carr, interview.

103. Driggars, "Musicians from Around Region."

104. Carr, interview.

High Plains Jamboree

105. BandsInTown, High Plains Jamboree, accessed October 31, 2022, https://www.bandsintown.com/a/11951780-high-plains-jamboree.

106. Jon Freeman, Chris Parton, Margaret Littman, Stephen L. Betts, Andrew Leahey and Joseph Hudak, "AmericanaFest 2016: 20 Best Things We Saw," *RollingStone*, September 26, 2016, https://www.rollingstone.com/music/music-country-lists/americanafest-2016-20-best-things-we-saw-110370/best-good-ole-days-high-plains-jamboree-111882.

107. Brian Kendall, "Between a Film and a New Album, Fort Worth Musician Simon Flory Talks Latest Projects," *Fort Worth Magazine*, April 8, 2021, https://fwtx.com/culture/burning-man.

108. Ibid.

The Lone Star Guitar Prodigy

109. Parker Jensen, email interview with the author, September 12, 2022.

Pickin' on the Square

110. Missy Raines, email interview with the author, September 26, 2022.

111. DeJean Miller, Zoom interview with the author, August 30, 2022.

112. Ibid.

113. Ibid.

114. Ibid.

115. Gary Penny, phone interview with the author, October 6, 2022.

116. Raines, interview.
117. Penny, interview.

Jade Throneberry's Full Plate

118. Jade Throneberry, interview with the author, October 3, 2022.
119. Ibid.
120. Ibid.

Play It Forward

121. Liner notes of the album *Scarecrow* by John Mellencamp.
122. Bluegrass Heritage Foundation, "Play It Forward," accessed November 25, 2022, https://bluegrassheritage.org/play-it-forward-free-youth-instrument-lending-program.

ABOUT THE AUTHORS

Braeden Paul and Jeff Campbell at the 2019 Bluegrass Heritage Festival in Farmers Branch, Texas. *Author's collection.*

Braeden Paul

Braeden Paul is a music reviewer, historian and musician. As a mandolinist, he has performed with multiple Dallas-based bands, including Blue Valley Bluegrass, Texas True and his own group, Braeden Paul & Wheel Hoss. He has even made guest appearances with professional artists such as Grammy award winner Michael Cleveland.

Braeden has contributed numerous music reviews to both *Bluegrass Today* and the Bluegrass Society of America. He has also coauthored the book *Texas Bluegrass History* (The History Press, 2021).

Braeden currently serves on the board of directors of the Southwest Bluegrass Club in Grapevine, Texas, and is also the founder of Braeden Paul's Bluegrass Preservation, a YouTube channel that showcases rare video and audio recordings of bluegrass and traditional acoustic music.

Jeff Campbell

Jeff Campbell is a historic preservationist, historian and museum professional. He has worked on historic preservation projects in Texas, Louisiana and New Mexico.

Jeff has written for *Plano Magazine*, Stephen F. Austin State University and Cowboy Poetry at the Bar D Ranch. He was also the winner of the 2011 Christmas Cowboy Poetry contest (Adult Division) from the National Cowgirl Museum and Hall of Fame. He is a featured artist on the Alan "The Black Ace" Kirby compilation CD *Teardrops to Reality*. Jeff is also a contributing poet in the book *Blue Ridge Parkway Celebrations*.

He has written the book *Murder and Mayhem on the Texas Rails* (History Press, 2022). Jeff has also coauthored *Texas Bluegrass History* (The History Press, 2021), *Hidden History of Plano, Texas* (The History Press, 2020), *Football and Integration in Plano, Texas: Stay in There, Wildcats!* (The History Press, 2014) and *Plano's Historic Cemeteries* (Arcadia Publishing, 2014).

Jeff considers himself a music lover but not a musician. However, he does play bass for the Fort Worth East Regional Library Band, jams with the Kanikapila Island Strummers, occasionally plays rhythm guitar with the Opihi Gang and teaches ukulele.